DRAMA CLASSICS

The Drama Classics sems to offer the world's greatest
plays in affordable pap
and theatregoers. The
introductions, unclutte
perspective.

Given that readers may be encountering a particular play
for the first time, the introduction seeks to fill in the
theatrical/historical background and to outline the chief
themes rather than concentrate on interpretational and
textual analysis. Similarly the play-texts themselves are free
of footnotes and other interpolations: instead there is an
end-glossary of 'difficult' words and phrases.

The texts of the English-language plays in the series
have been prepared taking full account of all existing
scholarship. The foreign-language plays have been newly
translated into a modern English that is both actable and
accurate: many of the translators regularly have their work
staged professionally.

Edited until his early death by Kenneth McLeish, the
Drama Classics series continues with his aim of providing a
first-class library of dramatic literature representing the best
of world theatre.

Associate editors:
Professor Trevor R. Griffiths
Professor in Humanities, University of Exeter
Dr Colin Counsell
Senior Lecturer in Theatre Studies and Performing Arts

DRAMA CLASSICS *the first hundred*

The Alchemist
All for Love
Andromache
Antigone
Bacchae
Bartholomew Fair
The Beaux Stratagem
The Beggar's Opera
Birds
Blood Wedding
The Changeling
A Chaste Maid in
    Cheapside
The Cherry Orchard
Children of the Sun
El Cid
The Country Wife
The Dance of Death
The Devil is an Ass
Doctor Faustus
A Doll's House
Don Juan
The Duchess of Malfi
Edward II
Electra (Euripides)
Electra (Sophocles)
An Enemy of the People
Everyman
The Father
Faust
A Flea in her Ear
Frogs
Fuente Ovejuna
The Game of Love
    and Chance
Ghosts
The Government
    Inspector
Hecuba
Hedda Gabler
The House of Bernarda
    Alba

The Hypochondriac
The Importance of
    Being Earnest
An Ideal Husband
An Italian Straw Hat
Ivanov
The Jew of Malta
The Knight of the
    Burning Pestle
The Lady from the Sea
The Learned Ladies
Lady Windermere's Fan
Life is a Dream
London Assurance
Lulu
Lysistrata
The Malcontent
The Man of Mode
The Marriage of Figaro
Mary Stuart
The Master Builder
Medea
The Misanthrope
The Miser
Miss Julie
A Month in the
    Country
Oedipus
The Oresteia
Peer Gynt
Phedra
The Playboy of the
    Western World
The Recruiting Officer
The Revenger's
    Tragedy
The Rivals
La Ronde
Rosmersholm
The Rover
Scapino
The School for Scandal

The Seagull
The Servant of Two
    Masters
She Stoops to Conquer
The Shoemakers'
    Holiday
Six Characters in
    Search of an
    Author
The Spanish Tragedy
Spring Awakening
Summerfolk
Tartuffe
Three Sisters
'Tis Pity She's a Whore
Too Clever by Half
Ubu
Uncle Vanya
Volpone
The Way of the World
The White Devil
The Widowing of Mrs
    Holroyd
The Wild Duck
A Woman Killed with
    Kindness
A Woman of No
    Importance
Women Beware Women
Women of Troy
Woyzeck
Yerma

*The publishers welcome
suggestions for further titles*

DRAMA CLASSICS

THE HOUSE OF BERNARDA ALBA

by

Federico García Lorca

translated and introduced by Jo Clifford

NICK HERN BOOKS

London

www.nickhernbooks.co.uk

A Drama Classic

The House of Bernarda Alba first published in Great Britain in this translation as a paperback original in 2012 by Nick Hern Books, The Glasshouse, 49a Goldhawk Road, London W12 8QP

Reprinted 2016

Copyright in the introduction © 2012 Nick Hern Books
Copyright in this translation © 2012 Jo Clifford

Jo Clifford has asserted her moral right to be identified as the translator of this work.

Typeset by Nick Hern Books, London
Printed by Mimeo Ltd, Huntingdon, Cambridgeshire PE29 6XX

A CIP catalogue record for this book is available from the British Library

ISBN 978 1 84842 181 3

Woodland CARBON
www.woodlandcarbon.co.uk
NICK HERN BOOKS
Printed on Carbon Captured paper

Introduction

Federico García Lorca (1898–1936)

Federico García Lorca was born on 5 June 1898. The year was a hugely significant one in Spanish cultural and political history: it gave its name to a whole generation of writers who used the events of this year as a rallying cry in efforts to convince the Spanish people of their country's deplorable state and the desperate need for re-evaluation and change. They were called the 'Generation of '98', and they included Azorín, Baroja and Ángel Ganivet.

The historical event that inspired this movement was the disastrous war with the United States, which led to the loss of Cuba, Spain's last remaining colony. This apparently distant event was to have huge repercussions for Lorca. Cuba had been Spain's principal source of sugar; Lorca's father was to be astute enough to plant his land in Southern Spain with sugar beet, and so, with the aid of a series of successful land purchases, he was well placed to become one of the richest men in the Fuente Vaqueros district.

A long-term consequence of this was that Lorca himself never needed to earn his own living. There's no question this wealthy background contributed both to the large volume, and the technical and emotional daring, of his work. As it happened, *Blood Wedding* in particular was hugely successful; but the financial security of his position left him absolutely free to write as he wanted without regard to the demands of the commercial theatre of his day.

However, the most immediate consequence for the young Lorca was that this meant he spent his childhood as the rich son of the wealthiest landowner of a mainly poor village.

Perhaps the best way for us to imagine the impact of this on Lorca's sensibility is to think of our own feelings towards the desperately poor of the developing world – or the homeless that many of us pass each day on the street. The contrast between his wealth and the poverty of so many of those around him left a deep impression on Lorca, which he was to express in later life in his autobiographical essay 'My Village'.

The plight of one family affected Lorca particularly deeply. One of his friends in the village was a little girl whose father was a chronically ill day-labourer and whose mother was the exhausted victim of countless pregnancies. The one day on which Federico was not allowed to visit their home was washing day: the members of this family had only one set of clothes, and they had to stay inside their house while their only clothes were being washed and dried. Lorca wrote:

> When I returned home on those occasions, I would look into the wardrobe, full of clean, fragrant clothes, and feel dreadfully anxious, with a dead weight on my heart.

He grew up with a profound sense of indignation at the injustice of this:

> No one dares to ask for what he needs. No one dares… to demand bread. And I who say this grew up among these thwarted lives. I protest against this mistreatment of those who work the land.

The young man who wrote this protest at the end of his adolescence maintained a profound anger right to the end of his life. In an interview he gave in 1936, the year of his death, he stated: 'As long as there is economic injustice in the world, the world will be unable to think clearly.'

He continued the interview with a fable to illustrate the difficulties of creating valid art in a situation of economic injustice:

> Two men are walking along a riverbank. One of them is rich, the other poor. One has a full belly and the other fouls the air with his yawns. And the rich man says: 'What a lovely little boat out on the water! Look at that lily blooming on the bank!' And the poor man wails: 'I'm hungry, so hungry!' Of course. The day when hunger is eradicated there is going to be the greatest spiritual explosion the world has ever seen. I'm talking like a real socialist, aren't I?

For Lorca, the art of creating theatre was totally bound up with the process of creating a better society:

> The idea of art for art's sake is something that would be cruel if it weren't, fortunately, so ridiculous. No decent person believes any longer in all that nonsense about pure art, art for art's sake. At this dramatic moment in time, the artist should laugh and cry with his people. We must put down the bouquet of lilies and bury ourselves up to the waist in mud to help those who are looking for lilies. For myself, I have a genuine need to communicate with others. That's why I knocked at the door of the theatre and why I now devote all my talents to it.

This passionate anger at the injustice of human society combined with an equally passionate determination to create art that might remedy it was fuelled not simply by his childhood experiences. As an adult, he had travelled to New York, and witnessed at first hand the devastating impact of the Wall Street Crash:

> It's the spectacle of all the world's money in all its splendour, its mad abandon and its cruelty... This is where I have got a clear idea of what a huge mass of people fighting to make money is really like. The truth is that it's an international war with just a thin veneer of courtesy... We ate breakfast on a thirty-second floor with the head of a bank, a charming person with a cold and feline side – quite English. People came in there after being paid. They were all counting dollars. Their hands all had the characteristic tremble that holding money gives them... Colin [an acquaintance] had five dollars in his purse and I three. Despite this he said to me: 'We're surrounded by millions and yet the only two decent people here are you and I.'

And when Lorca writes so angrily of the 'thwarted lives' of those whose existence is dominated by money, it is clear he is thinking not simply of the plight of the rural poor, but also of the bourgeoisie to which he himself, and many of us, now belong. He is concerned not simply with the suffering that a wealthy middle class inflicts on those beneath them on the social scale; he is equally concerned with the suffering they inflict upon themselves. The 'thwarted lives' he saw in his village are not simply those of the poor.

The House of Bernarda Alba: **What Happens in the Play**

Act One   Offstage, the bells are tolling for Bernarda's second husband's funeral. La Poncia, Bernarda's housekeeper, is eating a sausage she stole from the larder. The (unnamed) maid is scrubbing the floor. Both share a common hatred for Bernarda, who is tight-fisted and domineering. La Poncia has been working for her for thirty years, and dreams of the humiliations she would like to inflict on her in revenge. A major anxiety for both is that the house be spotlessly clean; and that Bernarda's mad mother, María Josefa, stay safely under lock and key.

La Poncia leaves to catch the last responses in church; the maid brutally repulses a hungry beggar woman, continues cleaning, cursing the dead man as she does so. It's the last time he'll molest her behind the stable door.

As Bernarda enters, she bursts into passionate weeping. The whole stage fills with women in black. In the midst of pious conversation, they gossip viciously behind Bernarda's back. Bernarda curses the women after they have gone. She lays down the law to her daughters: mourning will last for eight years. Eight years of utter seclusion.

But there is an immediate threat to her control: the eldest daughter, Angustias, has been seen watching the men through the house door's iron grille. Bernarda calls her in and slaps her. She sends her daughters off to their rooms; and La Poncia tells Bernarda the men were talking about a village girl who was gang-raped the previous night.

We have a strong sense of a world where the double standard rules: men are allowed free expression of their sexuality, while women must repress theirs.

Bernarda goes to see the lawyer to discuss the terms of her late husband's will.

As an act of rebellion, Adela, the youngest, has changed into a green dress. The other sisters talk of the rumour that Pepe el Romano, the most eligible bachelor of the district, is going to propose marriage to Angustias. Besides being the eldest, she is also the richest, because she inherits from her father, Bernarda's first husband. It becomes clear that Adela loves Pepe, and may be in a relationship with him, and that there is bitter rivalry between the sisters. The girls then rush off to catch a glimpse of Pepe walking down the street.

Bernarda sees Angustias with make-up on her face, and violently rubs it off. The sisters rush on to see what the conflict is. At that moment, María Josefa appears, dressed in faded finery. She's going to escape from this prison and live with a man by the shores of the sea. Bernarda and her daughters join to drag the mad, suffering old woman back into confinement.

Act Two   The sisters are doing their embroidery. All seems calm. Angustias's engagement to Pepe is now official. As custom dictates, he comes each night to converse with her through the metal grille of her window. Adela is in her room, alone; they all have noticed her agitation and distress. There is also an unexplained discrepancy around the time he leaves Angustias. She says it is around one a.m.; but others say he has been heard leaving at around four. The woman go off to see a travelling salesman who deals in lace.

Adela is left alone with La Poncia. She tells her she wants Pepe and means to have him. She will not allow anyone to stop her. La Poncia advises her to wait. Angustias is sickly and narrow-hipped. The first childbirth will kill her. Then Pepe will return for Adela. But Adela will not wait. It is clear she and Angustius are in a state of war.

The sisters return. It is midday. The heat suffocates. A gang of itinerant labourers have come to harvest the fields. They hired a prostitute the previous night. All hear them singing as they come back from the fields.

Angustias breaks the stillness in a state of fury. Someone has taken Pepe's photograph from her room. Bernarda orders La Poncia to search the girls' rooms. There is an expectation it will be found in Adela's; but it turns out it is the hunchbacked sister, Martirio, who has stolen it. Bernarda beats her, and there is an explosion of jealous fury betwen Martirio and Adela. Bernarda, in fury, sends the sisters back to their rooms.

Alone together, La Poncia hints to Bernarda about a scandal she suspects is about to break over Bernarda's head. Bernarda retaliates by reminding La Poncia of the knowledge she has of the scandal surrounding her – and fiercely asserts her confidence in her ability to control events. La Poncia artfully remarks that it's wonderful how keen Pepe is on his new fiancée, since he stays talking to her till four in the morning. Angustias denies this: Martirio corroborates it. We have a sense that the sisters have been overhearing everything; we know for sure that Adela has, in fact, been seeing Pepe; and we sense her secret is in danger of being revealed.

A tumult in the street diverts everyone's attention. Adela and Martirio snatch a moment together. Martirio also loves Pepe and is determined to prevent Adela having him. This is another declaration of open war.

The stage fills again as La La Poncia reveals what she has just heard: an unmarried girl in the village secretly gave birth to an illegitimate child and killed it to hide her shame. The village dogs uncovered the child's corpse from under a heap of stones. A mob is forming to lynch the mother. Adela clutches her belly. We know she is pregnant. Bernarda shouts at the mob to act fast before the police come – and urges them to kill the girl.

Act Three   All seems quiet again as the daughters eat their evening meal. Someone has come to visit; and from the woman's conventional words we catch a glimpse of a life lived in unresolved misery, whose anguish is tucked away out of sight – but never out of mind. The night is dark; the stars are big as fists; a stallion is trying to kick his way out of the stable.

Bernarda is sure she has the situation under control. But the talk between Bernarda and the maid after she has gone to bed suggests otherwise.

The Grandmother appears, singing to a baby lamb. Martirio persuades her back to bed in a scene of the profoundest fear and pathos. The hatred between Martirio and Adela is coming irresistibly out into the open, as is the fact that Adela and Pepe are having intercourse together. At a crucial moment of conflict between the two sisters, we hear a man whistle. It is Pepe; this is the signal for Adela to join him; Martirio prevents her leaving.

Martirio calls out for her mother. Bernarda appears. She moves to strike Adela. But Adela grabs her mother's stick and breaks it. Bernarda runs off for her rifle. We hear the gunshot. Martirio comes back on stage to say Pepe has been shot dead. She is lying. But Adela believes her and runs off, locking herself in her room.

Adela has hung herself. Bernarda orders her to be cut down. She orders her daughters to stop weeping. She announces to the world that her youngest daughter died a virgin. She imposes silence. The play ends.

Sources

When Lorca was still a boy, he sometimes spent the summers with his family in a small village called Asquerosa. Across the street lived a domineering woman called Frasquita Alba Sierra, who had married twice and had a total of seven children from her two marriages. Lorca's cousins lived across the street from him, next door to this woman's house. They shared a well with her at the back of their houses; much of what went on in the Alba household could be heard quite clearly and was passed onto the Lorcas – and in particular to the fascinated young Federico.

It is very clear that this household, with its domineering mother, its many daughters, their clashes with their mother over her authority, and their disputes about who would eventually inherit the family property, was the seed that, once planted in Federico's imagination as a boy, was finally to grow into *The House of Bernarda Alba* – this utterly extraordinary creation of the last months of his life. Indeed, the resemblance between the Frasquita Alba of the village and the Bernarda Alba of the play was so close that it horrified Lorca's mother. She begged him to change Bernarda's name so as not to offend the surviving members of Frasquita's family. One theory even has it that the animosity provoked by the resemblance between the names was so strong that it was one of the factors that led to Lorca's asassination.

Because he never lived long enough to revise the play or have it performed, we can only speculate as to whether he would have agreed to his mother's request. What is for sure, though, is that he took from his early memories of the village and its surroundings much more than the name and basic characteristics of this one household. The whole action of the play is rooted in the rural surroundings in which he grew up. In fact, in an early draft of the play, he described its setting as 'an Andalusian village on arid land'. This description precisely fits Asquerosa; and in many other respects the village of the play corresponds very closely to the village he knew as a child. 'Asquerosa' in Spanish means 'disgusting, loathsome', and in certain respects, at least, this seems to have been a place which lived up to its name. It was rife with gossip and with an utterly obsessive and often deeply damaging fascination with other people's lives; a place with a poisonous atmosphere, beautifully summed up by Bernarda herself where she talks of 'this wretched little village, without a river. This village of wells, where you're afraid to drink the water in case it's been poisoned.'

Many other details of life, as portrayed in the play, are authentic to the village: the incredibly long periods of mourning; the repressive sexual morality; the appalling, crushing heat; the arrival of the reapers in the summer from the hills. Even the language of the play is said to reflect the inhabitants' particular way of speaking. Many of the characters, too, are based on real people Lorca knew as a child. La Poncia was a real servant, although she never worked for Frasquita Alba. Bernarda's crazy old grandmother, María Josefa, was inspired by an aged relative Federico and his brother used to visit when they were children. The rejected suitor, Enrique Humanes, and the husband whose wife gets carried off to the olive grove were also people who existed in flesh and blood.

Adela's green dress was inspired by one of Lorca's favourite cousins, who also had a green dress she dearly loved and who, on one celebrated family occasion, could only show it off to the chickens in the backyard because the family was going through a period of mourning.

No doubt a more patient researcher could investigate many more incidents and characters in the play and discover many more links between them and Lorca's experience of life in the villages of Spain. And perhaps this is one of the reasons why Lorca prefaces the play with the words: 'The poet wishes to point out that these three acts are intended to be a photographic documentary.'

So before we even begin to experience the play we are invited to bear in mind that what it represents is actually true – on whatever level we may choose to interpret this. We may wonder why Lorca should choose such a subject: why so extraordinarily gifted and imaginative a poet should choose such an apparently unpoetic form.

It is certainly striking that Lorca should have chosen to return to these childhood roots after a life which, even the briefest summary indicates, took him far from his own roots in the Andalusian countryside. He left for Madrid when he was twenty-one, encountered the vibrant intellectual and artistic life of the capital, and had intense relationships with the film-maker Buñuel, the surrealist artist Salvador Dalí, and a dazzling group of young writers and poets. In 1928, the extraordinary success of his book of poems *The Gypsy Ballads* (*Romancero Gitano*) made him one of Spain's best-known poets. By 1929 he was in New York, where he witnessed the Wall Street Crash, and then made a triumphant lecture/recital tour of Cuba and South America. He was fascinated by surrealism, film-making, painting and jazz. Even this, the briefest of descriptions, should make it clear that this was a poet and artist open to influence from all over the globe. It is extraordinary that at the end of his life he should, in a sense, turn his back on all this and concentrate with an almost obsessive power and precision on scenes from his own childhood.

The House of Bernarda Alba, more than many of his other plays, is steeped in the personal, social and cultural contexts that helped shape it. To begin to understand it, we need to make an imaginative journey back into the author's past and, through that journey, make the connections that help us understand this play in the present.

Social Concerns

The wealthiest character in this play is perhaps also the one most thwarted in her life; and who, as a consequence, passionately devotes herself to thwarting the lives of others. Like the head of a Wall Street bank, Bernarda is portrayed as someone whose animal greed and savagery is only thinly masked by a veneer of conventional piety. She works constantly to increase her material wealth, as her neighbours' remarks reveal, and her avarice lies at the heart of the suffering she inflicts on herself and on others. It is a side of Bernarda that has been cannily perceived by the mad old María Josefa in her little rhyme: 'Bernarda's got a leopard's face'.

The comparative wealth possessed by the Alba family brings them no happiness. Instead, both mother and daughters seem trapped in a cage of their own making, in which they remain imprisoned by their own fear and their own sense of class values. This snobbery denies them any slight avenues of escape – such as marriage to Enrique Humanas for Martirio. Adela is the only one with the courage to attempt to break free: and that courage costs her her life.

The Play's Religious Dimension

When Lorca was a child, he was fascinated by the village church, and by its (still semi-pagan) festivals – one of which was the starting point for his earlier tragedy *Yerma*. Behind the church altar was a smiling image of the Virgin of Good Love (La Virgen del Buen Amor):

When the organ started up my soul was in ecstasy and I fixed my eyes tenderly on the child Jesus and the Virgin of Good Love, always loving and a little silly with her tin crown, stars and spangles. When the organ started up, the smoke of the incense and the tinkling of the little bells excited me, and I would become terrified of sins which no longer concern me.

His fascination with religion spilled over into the games Lorca used to play at home. A childhood friend remembered how he created a little shrine to the Virgin in the backyard of his house, decorated it with flowers from the garden, dressed up in a variety of finery from the dressing-up box in the attic and pretended to say mass to family and friends with the most profound conviction. The climax of the service was his sermon: and he insisted that everyone cried.

Lorca retained a profound concern with religion throughout his life, though as he grew older he came to detest many aspects of the Catholic Church; a rage that was to attain magnificent expression in the poem 'Cry to Rome'. This is an amazing denunciation not only of the savage cruelty and inhumanity of the capitalist system Lorca saw operating in New York, but of the complacency of a Catholic Church that refuses to disengage itself from such corruption and which has, in consequence, utterly lost touch with its spirituality.

A similar rage informs the church imagery used in *The House of Bernarda Alba*. The play begins with a church service, whose bells are heard offstage. But the tinkling of little bells that aroused the soul of the young Lorca to ecstasy have here been transformed into a heavy symbol of physical and emotional repression:

Bloody bells! Going round and round my head!

The very first line spoken in the play, then, sets the scene for a kind of distorted Passion Play whose central figure, Bernarda, a kind of Virgin of Bad Love, destroys the sexuality and the lives of herself and all around her. She presides over a house which La Poncia significantly refers to as a 'convent' – a convent dedicated not to the love of God or concern for mankind but to cruelty and repression masquerading as a kind of sacrilegious piety.

By this late stage in his career, Lorca's loathing for reactionary elements in the Catholic Church had become reciprocal; following the opening of his play *Yerma* in 1934, Lorca had come to be viewed as an enemy of the church. There's no question that his targets in *Bernarda Alba* were those same repressive Church authorities enjoying and abusing a centuries-old position of privilege.

He presents us, in *The House of Bernarda Alba*, with a world dominated by piety at its most oppressive; Christ, however, is not altogether absent from this world. Adela expresses her final act of rebellion in terms which powerfully remind us of his passion:

Even if all the so-called respectable people in this so-called respectable village pursue me and hunt me down, I'll still stand by him. Openly and without shame. And I'll gladly wear my crown of thorns.

This deliberate association of sexual freedom with the figure of Jesus Christ is something that must continue to shock the conservatively minded. In his own imagination, perhaps, Lorca is still dressed as a priest, preaching a sermon: a sermon of human liberation.

The House of Bernarda Alba on Stage

The first public performance of *The House of Bernarda Alba* took place on 8 March 1945 in the Teatro Avenida in Buenos Aires, where it was performed by Margarita Xirgu and her company. It was, however, another nineteen years before it became possible to get it past the censors of Franco's Spain and was performed in Madrid on 10 January 1964 at the Teatre Goya.

Since then it has gone on to become one of the most-often performed of Lorca's plays, and its theatrical history has been skilfully summarised in Maria Delgado's excellent study of Lorca as a dramatist.

Notable productons in Spain include Calixto Bieito's abstract staging for Madrid's Centro Dramático Nacional in 1998. He set the play in an austere, empty space, dominated by chairs, and overhung by a nude aerialist whose contortions counterpointed the protagonists' sexual frustrations.

In many respects the play's dramatic world is intensely alien to the world of British theatre, and this presents many difficulties to stagings of the play in English. It's very easy, for instance, for English-language productions to get themselves tangled up in the British class system. Hard to convey Bernarda's upper-class pretensions without sounding terribly Home Counties; difficult to convey the searing heat of the house's interior in chilly British springs and summers; perhaps impossible to convey to an urban British audience the restrictions placed on rural Spanish women's lives.

None of this has prevented many different productions on the British stage. Perhaps the most celebrated English-language production took place in the Lyric Theatre Hammersmith in the early 1980s. Translated by Robert David MacDonald and directed by Nuria Espert, it starred Joan Plowright and Glenda Jackson in the leading roles, was immensely successful and transferred to the West End.

Polly Teale's staging of Rona Munro's version for Shared Experience in 1999 took the play on a wide-ranging English tour that opened in Salisbury and played throughout the country before ending up in London's Young Vic.

In spite of the difficulties, which English-language productions have arguably never fully resolved, the play has a visceral resonance and power that mean it continually cries out to be staged.

To Conclude

Lorca once said that you could judge the health of a nation's culture by looking at the state of its theatre. And for him theatre was a natural extension of poetry: a poetry that leaps off the printed page, escapes from between the pages of books 'and becomes human. It shouts and speaks. It cries and despairs.'

For Lorca there was nothing precious about poetry; it was simply part of living. He once wrote: 'Poetry is something that just walks along the street.'

Because for him it was a part of living, to be deprived of it was a kind of torment; and to deprive people of the chance of experiencing it was a kind of crime. In an interview he gave to an English journalist, he spoke of his anger at the lack of theatre that was the norm in Spain outside the capital:

> Theatre is almost dead outside Madrid, and the people suffer accordingly, as they would if they had lost eyes or ears or sense of taste.

He also said, 'I will always be on the side of those who have nothing.' He was a political writer in the deepest sense, in that the act of writing was part of the struggle for a better world.

> Sometimes, when I think of what is going on in the world, I wonder why am I writing? The answer is that one simply has to work. Work and go on working. Work and help everyone who deserves it. Work even though at times it feels like so much wasted effort. Work as a form of protest. For one's impulse has to be to cry out every day one wakes up and is confronted by misery and injustice of every kind: 'I protest! I protest! I protest!'

All these concerns came together in Lorca's work for La Barraca, the travelling theatre he helped to found in the early years of the Republic. They would set up a simple stage in the town square and perform the great, and then almost completely neglected, classics of the Spanish theatre – the works of Lope de Vega, Tirso de Molina and Calderón.

His work on this incredibly bold and imaginative precursor of our own small-scale touring companies had a profound effect on Lorca. Experiencing the impact these classics made on a mass audience was a source of strength and inspiration; and working on the texts themselves must surely have deepened his remarkable theatre-writing skills.

These skills are astonishingly present in every word of *The House of Bernarda Alba*. Lorca wrote of it, 'I've had to cut a lot of things in this tragedy. I cut out a lot of facile songs and little rhymes. I want the work to have a severe simplicity.' The dialogue is of an incredible economy and power; its emotional intensity is such that just reading it in the Spanish is enough to send shivers up the spine. Perhaps even more remarkable is the immaculate structure that underpins the dialogue; the way he has imperceptibly telescoped events that would normally have taken a few weeks, without losing that sense of urgency and speed that great tragedy demands.

He wrote it for the very great actress, Margarita Xirgu, with whom he had collaborated over many years and for whom he wrote so much of his work: *Mariana Pineda, Doña Rosita the Spinster, Blood Wedding, Yerma*. If you write for the theatre, inevitably you are influenced by who you are writing for; there is no question about the fact that Xirgu must have influenced Lorca and been at least partly responsible for the amazing range of excellent female parts he wrote for the stage.

Lorca was also a homosexual, who had the misfortune to live in a country where, and at a time when, male homosexuality was considered deeply shameful. He was denied the right to express his sexuality openly in his life; denied, too, the right to explore it or express it openly in his work. It seems very obvious that the grotesquely unjust and unnecessary suffering he had to endure as a result deepened his own identification with women denied control over their own bodies and access to their own sexuality.

In *Bernarda Alba* this oppression is seen at its most extreme. Lorca warned that the play should not just be taken as a metaphor; another reason why he wrote on the title page that the play should be considered a 'photographic documentary'.

At first sight, he seems to be presenting us with a very remote and alien world, but the worst mistake we could make, either in watching or presenting it, would be to treat it as a kind of curiosity, the theatrical equivalent of a tourist trip to an exotic location. For all of us have our Bernarda somewhere inside us: our own monstrous tyrant of conformity and shame that inhibits so much of our human and creative impulse.

Lorca finished the play in the summer of 1936; he read it aloud to friends, as was his custom, and then left Madrid for his habitual summer vacation in his home town of Granada. He took the manuscript with him, along with the toy theatre that he took everywhere on his travels. He was mildly worried about how the play would be received, and how people would take the fact that it had no men in it. He had written one of the truly great works of this century; it is oddly endearing to find him worried about it.

He intended to revise it, but never had the time. Civil war broke out, the fascist authorities took him away and had him shot. He was thirty-eight years old. For, as Lorca was writing the play, an army general called Francisco Franco, with his head stuffed with dead ideas, was preparing a revolution. Lorca may not have consciously known it, but he was writing under the shadow of death.

All of us now watching *Bernarda Alba* watch under a shadow of our own. Authorities parrot nonsense at us, dazzle us with intellectually void and morally bankrupt talk of 'profitability' and 'enterprise'. Old and moribund ideas, ideas which should have died with the nineteenth century, still haunt us and threaten our environment and our lives, even if they are dressed up with words like 'modernisation'. We may imagine the threat to be remote. So did Lorca. Threats have a habit of seeming unreal until it is too late to avert them. We have to take the play as a warning: we have to learn.

Note

The present translation was first presented at the Royal Lyceum Theatre in Edinburgh in May 1989 and has been revised for publication here.

Lorca: Key Dates

1898   5 June, Federico García Lorca born in Fuente Vaqueros, near Granada, Spain.

1909   His family move to Granada.

1914   Lorca enters Granada University to study law, on his father's insistence. Lorca had wanted to study music.

1919   Lorca enters the Residencia de Estudiantes in Madrid.

1920   Lorca's first play, *The Butterfly's Evil Spell*, opens in Madrid. It is a catastrophic failure.

1921   Publication of Lorca's first book of poems, *Libro de poemas*.

1922   The painter, Salvador Dalí, then eighteen, arrives in Madrid. He and Lorca become close friends.

1924–5   Lorca completes two more plays: *Mariana Pineda* and *The Shoemaker's Amazing Wife*.

1927   *Mariana Pineda* finally produced. An astonishing success.

1928   Publication of *Gypsy Ballads*.

1929   *The Love of Don Perlimplín* is about to be produced in Madrid, but the theatre is closed by the dictatorship.

Lorca leaves for New York, where he witnesses the Wall Street Crash.

1930   Lorca returns to Spain via Cuba.

1931   Collapse of the dictatorship: establishment of the Spanish Republic.

1932   Lorca sets up La Barraca theatre company and begins touring the villages of Spain with productions of plays by Lope de Vega, Tirso de Molina and Calderón.

1933   Triumphant first production of *Blood Wedding*. Hitler comes to power in Germany.

1933–4 Lorca visits Argentina, where his work is triumphantly received.

1934   Opening night of *Yerma* scandalises right-wing and traditional Catholic opinion.

1936   Successful opening of his play *Doña Rosita the Spinster*. Growing political unrest in Spain. Lorca writes *The House of Bernarda Alba*.

14 July, returns to his parents in Granada.

17 July, reads *The House of Bernarda Alba* to his friends in Granada.

18 July, rebel right-wing uprising led by General Franco marks beginning of Civil War.

23 July, right-wing rebels take over Granada.

18 August, Federico García Lorca murdered by fascists.

For Further Reading

The best guide to Lorca's life is Ian Gibson's magnificent biography: *Federico García Lorca: A Life*, Faber, 1989.

His brother's memoir has been translated by Christopher Maurer: *In the Green Morning: Memories of Federico, by Francisco García Lorca*, Peter Owen, 1989.

A good academic introduction to Lorca's plays is Gwynne Edwards' *The Theatre Beneath the Sand*, Marion Boyars, 1989.

An excellent contemporary introduction to his work as a dramatist is Maria M. Delgado's *Federico García Lorca*, Routledge Modern and Contemporary Dramatists, London, 2008.

Gay themes in Lorca's work are explored in *Lorca and the Gay Imagination* by Paul Binding, GMP Books, 1985.

There are a great many available translations of Lorca's poetry. One of the best is *Poet in New York* (bilingual edition), translated by Greg Simon and Steven F. White, Viking, 1988.

An interesting collection of essays and creative responses, including discussions of the problems of translating Lorca is *Fire, Blood and the Alphabet: One Hundred Years of Lorca*, ed. Doggart and Thompson, Durham University Press, 2000.

THE HOUSE OF BERNARDA ALBA

Characters

BERNARDA ALBA, *sixty years old*
MARÍA JOSEFA, *eighty years old, her mother*
ANGUSTIAS, *thirty-nine years old, her daughter*
MAGDALENA, *thirty years old, her daughter*
AMELIA, *twenty-seven years old, her daughter*
MARTIRIO, *twenty-four years old, her daughter*
ADELA, *twenty years old, her daughter*
LA PONCIA, *sixty years old, a servant*
MAID, *fifty years old*
PRUDENCIA, *fifty years old*
BEGGAR WOMAN
FIRST WOMAN
SECOND WOMAN
THIRD WOMAN
FOURTH WOMAN
GIRL
WOMEN IN MOURNING

The poet wishes to point out that these three acts are intended to be a photographic documentary.

ACT ONE

A blindingly white room inside BERNARDA ALBA's *house. The walls are thick. There are arched doorways with hessian curtains, edged with tassels and flounces. Cane chairs. On the walls are pictures of unlikely landscapes full of nymphs or legendary kings. It is summer. A heavy silence. We are deep in shadow. As the curtain rises, the stage is empty. We hear the tolling of a funeral bell.*

Enter the MAID.

MAID. Bloody bells! Going round and round my head!

LA PONCIA (*enters eating bread and chorizo*). Two hours of gibberish and they're still at it. And all to bury an old fart. May he rest in peace. The place is swarming with priests. Still. The church looks lovely. Magdalena fainted at the first paternoster.

MAID. Poor thing. She'll miss him.

LA PONCIA. She was the only one the old man cared about. Still. At least we got a minute to ourselves. I was hungry.

MAID. What if she saw you?

LA PONCIA. Herself? Domineering old bitch! You know, just because she's not eating, she'd like to see the rest of us die of hunger. Still. She can go to hell. I just felt like a sausage.

MAID (*with an anxious eagerness*). Could you give me
something for my little girl?

LA PONCIA. Take a few beans. No one'll notice.

MARÍA JOSEFA (*within*). Bernarda!

LA PONCIA. Have you got her well locked up?

MAID. I turned both the keys.

LA PONCIA. You should have put the bolt across as well.
That old dear can pick locks with her fingers.

MARÍA JOSEFA. Bernarda!

LA PONCIA (*shouts*). She's coming! (*To the* MAID.) You make
sure everything's clean. If Bernarda finds one thing she
can't see her face in she'll tear out the few hairs I've got left.

MAID. What a woman! What a woman!

LA PONCIA. She's like an empress. She who must be
obeyed. Do you know what she'd like to do? She'd like to
sit on your heart and slowly squeeze the life out of it.
She'd take a whole year to do it, and she'd just sit there,
like on a throne, just watching you gasping for air. She'd
just sit and watch you and smile. Her cold cold smile.
That cup's filthy.

MAID. I've been scrubbing all day. My hands are bleeding.

LA PONCIA. She wants her house to be the cleanest, her
manners to be the nicest, herself to be the highest class.
It's her husband I felt sorry for. I expect he's glad to be
dead. Got shut of her anyway.

The bells stop ringing.

MAID. Has all the family come?

LA PONCIA. Just hers. His people came to see his corpse.
They just filed in, crossed themselves, and filed out again.
They can't stand the sight of her.

MAID. Have we got enough chairs?

LA PONCIA. Probably. If not, they'll just have to sit on the
floor. You know, since her father died she's not let a soul
into the house. It's her little empire, and she doesn't want
anyone else to see it. Tight-fisted old bitch!

MAID. She's always been good to you.

LA PONCIA. Thirty years I've worked for her. Thirty years
washing her sheets. Thirty years scrubbing her floors.
Eating her leftovers. Up all night when she coughs.
Spending days on end with my ears glued to the walls.
Just so I could bring her back some titbit of gossip she
could blackmail the neighbours with. Thirty years of my
life given up to her. And we've no secrets from each
other. She's like an open book to me. And I hate her guts.
I'd like to tear out her eyes and nail them to the
doorpost.

MAID. That's terrible.

LA PONCIA. But don't worry. I'm a good bitch. I'm like
her little dog who barks when she tells me to and snaps
at the heels of the beggars when she sets me onto them.
I've worked for her all my life and my sons work her
land and they're married but one day I'll have had
enough. One day.

MAID. And then what?

LA PONCIA. And then I'll lock myself in a room with her and throw away the key. I'll spit in her face for a year and by the time I've finished with her she'll look like one of those lizards the little boys torment in the streets. The kind they pick up and pull the legs off one by one. Not that I envy her. All she's been left with is five ugly daughters with not a penny to their name. Except the eldest. Angustias. And the only reason she's got money is because she's the daughter of the first husband. And he was rich. As for the others, they've got loads of fancy needlework, loads of lace on their underskirts but nothing when she dies. Nothing but dry bread and sour grapes.

MAID. I wish I had what they've got.

LA PONCIA. All we've got is our hands to work with and a hole to be buried in.

MAID. That's all we have. All they ever let us have.

LA PONCIA (*at the glass cupboard*). This is filthy.

MAID. I've tried soaking it. I've tried scrubbing it. The stains won't come out.

The bells ring.

LA PONCIA. That'll be them finishing. I think I'll go and listen. The best bit's always at the end. And that priest's got a lovely voice. In the paternoster it just went up and up and up. Like water filling a jar. Course, he fluffed it in the end, but it was good while it lasted. The only one who could do a good 'Amen' was the old sacristan. Tronchapinos. I used to love to hear him. I remember him at my mother's funeral, may she rest in peace. He made the walls shake. It sounded like there was a wolf in the church. (*Imitating him.*) Ameeeeeeen! (*Starts to cough.*)

MAID. You'll strain your voice.

LA PONCIA. I'd rather be straining something else! (*Exits, laughing.*)

The MAID *cleans. Bells ring.*

MAID. Ding ding dong. Ding ding dong. God forgive him.

BEGGAR WOMAN (*with a child*). Glory be to God.

MAID. Ding ding dong. God give him peace.

BEGGAR WOMAN (*louder, and with a certain irritation*). Glory be to God!

MAID (*annoyed*). And on earth peace and goodwill!

BEGGAR WOMAN. I've come for the leftovers.

MAID. See that door? It leads out to the street. Today's leftovers are for me.

BEGGAR WOMAN. It's all right for you. You get paid. Me and my child get nothing. We're alone in the world.

MAID. So are the dogs. They're alone in the world too. Doesn't do them any harm.

BEGGAR WOMAN. But I always get the leftovers.

MAID. Get out of here. Who said you could come in? Get out. You've left dirty footmarks all over my clean floor.

They go. The MAID *cleans.*

This house. This house where they use olive oil to polish the floors. This house with its mahogany cupboards and its fancy chairs. With its fine linen and brass bedsteads. Just so we can live in mud huts with our one tin plate and worn-out spoon. I hope the day comes when it's all burnt to the ground!

The bells start to ring.

You and your bells! You in your walnut coffin with its gilt handles and silken ropes to carry it! You're just the same as us now. No better off than us. Antonio María Benavides. Lying there in your stiff collar and your creaky boots. That's the last time you touch me up behind the stable door.

From the back, WOMEN IN MOURNING *start to enter, two by two. They wear black headscarves, long black skirts, and carry black fans. They slowly enter until they fill the stage.*

(*Bursting into tears.*) Antonio María Benavides! You will never come through that door again! Never see these walls or eat bread at your own table! I loved you more than anyone else who served you. (*Tearing her hair.*) How can I live now you have gone?

The two hundred WOMEN *have all come in.* BERNARDA *appears with her five* DAUGHTERS. BERNARDA *leans on a stick.*

BERNARDA (*to the* MAID). Silence!

MAID (*crying*). Bernarda!

BERNARDA. Less tears. More work. The house is filthy. Everything should have been spotless for the mourners. Now get out. This is not your place.

The MAID *goes out, sobbing.*

The poor are like animals. They are not in the least like us.

FIRST WOMAN. The poor also feel pain.

BERNARDA. They forget it when they see a plate of beans.

GIRL (*timidly*). One must eat to live.

BERNARDA. At your age I never spoke in front of my elders.

FIRST WOMAN. Be quiet, girl.

BERNARDA. No one has ever had to teach me my manners. Sit.

They sit. Pause.

(*Loudly.*) Don't cry, Magdalena. If you must cry go and do it under the bed. Do you hear me?

SECOND WOMAN. Has the threshing started?

BERNARDA. Yesterday.

THIRD WOMAN. The sun is heavy as lead.

SECOND WOMAN. I've never known such heat.

Pause. They all fan themselves.

BERNARDA. Is the lemon juice ready?

LA PONCIA *enters with a big tray of little white glasses, which she hands out.*

LA PONCIA. Yes, Bernarda.

BERNARDA. Give some to the men.

LA PONCIA. I've given them theirs already. They're drinking it out in the yard.

BERNARDA. Make sure they go out the same way they came in. I don't want them in the house.

GIRL (*to* ANGUSTIUS). Pepe el Romano was there.

ANGUSTIAS. I saw him.

BERNARDA. She saw his mother. His mother was there.
Not Pepe. She never saw Pepe and neither did I.

GIRL. But I thought…

BERNARDA. There was one man there. An old man. The
widower of Darajalí. He was there. Standing next to your
aunt. We all saw him.

SECOND WOMAN (*aside, in a low voice*). She's got a vicious
tongue!

THIRD WOMAN (*aside, in a low voice*). Sharp as a razor!

BERNARDA. The only man women should look at in
church is the priest. And only because he wears a skirt. To
look at any other man is to act like a bitch on heat.

FIRST WOMAN (*aside, in a low voice*). She's half on heat
herself.

LA PONCIA (*between her teeth*). And devious with it.

BERNARDA (*striking the floor with her stick*). God be praised.

ALL (*crossing themselves*). May He be blessed and praised for
ever.

BERNARDA. May His servant rest in peace
With Angels and Archangels
And all the Holy Company of Heaven.

ALL. May he rest in peace.

BERNARDA. May St Michael watch over him
With his sharp and terrible sword.

ALL. May he rest in peace.

BERNARDA. May St Peter open doors to him
   With the key that opens Heaven and closes Hell.

ALL. May he rest in peace.

BERNARDA. May he dwell with the souls of the blessed
   and the little spirits who light up the fields.

ALL. May he rest in peace.

BERNARDA. With the souls who die in holy charity
   With the souls who watch over land and sea.

ALL. May he rest in peace.

BERNARDA. God give eternal rest to your servant Antonio
   María Benavides and give him the crown of your eternal
   glory.

ALL. Amen.

BERNARDA (*stands up and sings*). *Requiem aeterna dona eis,
   Domine.*

ALL (*on their feet and chanting a Gregorian chant*). *Et lux perpetua
   luceat eis.*

   They all cross themselves.

FIRST WOMAN. God give you health to pray for his soul.

   They start filing out.

THIRD WOMAN. May you always have bread to bake in
   your oven.

SECOND WOMAN. And a roof to shelter you and your
   children.

They all file past in front of BERNARDA *and exit. Exit* ANGUSTIUS *through another door, which leads to the yard.*

FOURTH WOMAN. May each day bring you joy; each day be like the day of your wedding.

LA PONCIA (*entering with a purse*). The men have collected this money for you to pay the priest for prayers.

BERNARDA. Thank them and give them brandy.

GIRL (*to* MAGDALENA). Magdalena.

BERNARDA (*to* MAGDALENA, *who starts to cry*). Ssssshhhh.

She hits the floor with her stick. Almost everyone has left.

(*To those who have gone.*) Go back to your caves! Back to your mud huts to criticise everything you've seen! I hope it's years before you darken my doors again!

LA PONCIA. You've got no right to complain. The whole village came.

BERNARDA. Yes, they came. To fill the house with sweat of their underskirts and the poison of their tongues.

AMELIA. Mother, don't talk like that!

BERNARDA. There's no other way of talking. Not about this wretched little village, without a river. This village of wells, where you're afraid to drink the water in case it's been poisoned.

LA PONCIA. What a state they've left the floor in!

BERNARDA. They've trampled all over it like a herd of goats.

LA PONCIA cleans the floor.

Daughter, give me a fan.

ADELA. Here's one.

She gives her a round fan decorated with red and green flowers.

BERNARDA (*throwing the fan to the ground*). Is this a fan to give a widow? Fans must be black. Learn to respect your father's memory.

MARTIRIO. Take mine.

BERNARDA. Won't you be hot?

MARTIRIO. I am never hot.

BERNARDA. You will be. We will brick up the doors and board up the windows. We won't let in a breath of air from the street. That's what happened in my father's house and in my father's father's house. Mourning will last for eight years. You will spend your days sewing. I have twenty chests of linen you will sew into sheets. Magdalena can embroider them. They will be for your trousseaux.

MAGDALENA. It's all the same to me.

ADELA (*bitter*). If you don't feel like doing it, then don't bother. Ours won't get embroidered, that's all. And you might get a better husband.

MAGDALENA. It won't make any difference. I'll never get married, I know that. I'd do anything rather than that. I'd rather sweep the streets. Anything rather than sit day after day in this dark room.

BERNARDA. That is what it is to be a woman.

MAGDALENA. Then women are cursed.

BERNARDA. Cursed or not, you do as I say. No use running to your father now. He can't help you any more. Needle and thread for females. Mule and whip for the man. That is the fate of people of substance.

Exit ADELA.

MARÍA JOSEFA (*off*). Bernarda, let me out!

BERNARDA (*shouts*). Let her go!

Enter the MAID.

MAID. It was hard work holding her down. She may be eighty, but she's as strong as an ox.

BERNARDA. My grandmother was the same. Strength runs in the family.

MAID. I had to gag her this morning. I stuffed an old sack in her mouth to stop her shouting about the washing-up water you give her to drink and the dog food you give her to eat. She says that's all she gets.

MARTIRIO. She's wicked.

BERNARDA (*to the* MAID). Let her run about in the yard.

MAID. She insisted on opening her old trunk and getting out all her jewels. Now she's put them all on and she says she's going to get married.

The DAUGHTERS *laugh.*

BERNARDA. Stay with her. Make sure she doesn't go near the well.

MAID. Are you worried in case she throws herself in?

BERNARDA. No. But it's the one spot in the yard where the neighbours can see her.

Exit the MAID.

MARTIRIO. We're going to change.

BERNARDA. You may. But not your headscarves.

Enter ADELA.

Where's Angustias?

ADELA (*in a sarcastic tone of voice*). Peeking at the men through a crack in the gate.

BERNARDA. And what were you doing there, may I ask?

ADELA. I wanted to make sure the hens were safe.

BERNARDA. Besides, the men have gone.

ADELA (*nastily*). There was still a group of them hanging about.

BERNARDA (*furious*). Angustias! Angustias!

ANGUSTIAS (*coming in*). Do you want something?

BERNARDA. Who were you looking at?

ANGUSTIAS. No one.

BERNARDA. Do you think it decent for a woman of your class to go running after men the day of her father's funeral? Answer me! Who were you looking at?

Pause.

ANGUSTIAS. I... I was looking at...

BERNARDA. Who?

ANGUSTIAS. No one!

BERNARDA (*advancing on her with her stick*). You sweet-tongued liar!

BERNARDA *hits* ANGUSTIAS.

LA PONCIA (*running in*). Bernarda, calm down!

She holds BERNARDA *back from* ANGUSTIAS. ANGUSTIAS *cries.*

BERNARDA. All of you, get out!

They leave.

LA PONCIA. She shouldn't have done it, I know. It was bad. But I don't think she really understood. Still. I was shocked to see her sidling off to the yard! There she was behind the window listening to the men's talk. Filth, of course. None of it worth listening to.

BERNARDA. That's all they come to funerals for! (*With avid curiosity.*) What did they talk about?

LA PONCIA. Paca la Roseta. Last night they tied her husband to a cattle trough and took her off to the olive grove.

BERNARDA. Did she resist?

LA PONCIA. Her? She enjoyed it. They say she rode along with her breasts hanging out and Maximiliano was playing her like a guitar. It doesn't bear thinking about!

BERNARDA. And then what happened?

LA PONCIA. What had to happen. They all came back just before dawn. Her hair was loose and she wore a wreath of flowers.

BERNARDA. She is the only bad woman in the village.

LA PONCIA. That's because she doesn't come from here. She comes from far away. And all the men who went with her are strangers too. Men from here would never do a thing like that.

BERNARDA. Of course not. But they like to hear about it just the same. And talk about it. And drool over it too.

LA PONCIA. That wasn't the only thing they spoke about.

BERNARDA (*looking from side to side a little fearfully*). What else did they talk about?

LA PONCIA. I can't tell you. I'd be too ashamed.

BERNARDA. And my daughter heard it all?

LA PONCIA. Of course!

BERNARDA. She takes after her aunts. She's sweet and white and slimy and she's got eyes like a sheep. All she wants to do is flirt with any little tradesman who takes her fancy. God knows how one has to struggle to make sure one's people grow up half-decent! How one has to suffer to stop them running wild!

LA PONCIA. Your daughters give you precious little trouble. And they're surely old enough now to look after themselves. Angustias must be well over thirty.

BERNARDA. She's just thirty-nine.

LA PONCIA. Imagine that. And she's never had a boyfriend.

BERNARDA (*furious*). And why should she have? Why should any of them? They get on very well without!

LA PONCIA. I'm sure I never meant to hurt your feelings.

BERNARDA. There's no one within a hundred miles of here who can touch them. The men here are simply not of their class. Do you want me to hand them over to some farmhand?

LA PONCIA. You could have looked in another village.

BERNARDA. Oh yes, and sold them!

LA PONCIA. No, Bernarda. Not sold them. Married them... Of course, in other places it might be you who'd look poor!

BERNARDA. Shut that vicious mouth of yours!

LA PONCIA. It's impossible to talk to you. Do we or do we not trust each other?

BERNARDA. We do not. You work for me. I pay you. That is all!

MAID (*entering*). Here's the lawyer to sort out the will.

BERNARDA. I'm coming. (*To the* MAID.) You whitewash the yard. (*To* LA PONCIA.) And you pack away all the dead man's clothes.

LA PONCIA. Perhaps we could give some things away.

BERNARDA. No. Nothing. Not a button! Not even the handkerchief we used to cover his face!

She exits slowly, leaning on her stick, and as she leaves she suddenly turns back to look at her servants. They leave after her.

Enter AMELIA *and* MARTIRIO.

AMELIA. Did you take your medicine?

MARTIRIO. It won't do me any good.

AMELIA. But did you take it?

MARTIRIO. Yes, I took it. On time. Like I do everything. Like clockwork.

AMELIA. You've looked better since that new doctor came.

MARTIRIO. I feel just the same.

AMELIA. Did you see? Adelaida wasn't at the service.

MARTIRIO. That doesn't surprise me. Her husband won't even let her out the door. She used to be so cheerful. Now she's always miserable.

AMELIA. I used to think things got better when you had a man. Now I don't know any more.

MARTIRIO. It doesn't make any difference.

AMELIA. What makes it so bad is all this endless gossip. It never lets us live. Poor Adelaida. It's really made her suffer.

MARTIRIO. She's terrified of Mother. She's the only one who knows the story of her father. And every time Adelaida's come, Mother's stuck the knife in. Her father went to Cuba and killed a man so he could marry his wife. And then he left her to run off with this other woman who had a daughter. And when he got tired of the mother, he ran off with the daughter. The mother went mad. She killed herself and he married the daughter. And she's Adelaida's mother.

AMELIA. The man's a criminal. Why hasn't he been locked up?

MARTIRIO. Because men always stick up for each other. Because they always cover up things like this and none of them has the guts to speak out.

AMELIA. And anyway, it's not Adelaida's fault.

MARTIRIO. No, but history has a habit of repeating itself. That's all life is. Things repeating themselves. I can see it now. And what'll happen to her will be the same as what happened to her mother and her grandmother. And they were both her father's wives.

AMELIA. It doesn't bear thinking about.

MARTIRIO. It's better never to see a man. I've been afraid of them ever since I was a little girl. I used to watch them as they yoked the oxen or carried the sacks of corn. They always used to shout and kick, I was always afraid of growing up in case one of them suddenly picked me up in his arms. Anyway, God has made me weak and ugly and set them completely apart from me.

AMELIA. Don't say such things! Enrique Humanes was after you. He liked you.

MARTIRIO. That was something people made up! Once I stood in my shift at the window. I stood there all night, waiting. Someone had told me he was coming, but he never came. It had just been talk. And then he married someone else. Someone who had more money.

AMELIA. And who was ugly as sin!

MARTIRIO. That doesn't bother them! All they care about is their oxen and their land and some submissive little creature to cook their food.

AMELIA (*sighs*). You're right!

Enter MAGDALENA.

MAGDALENA. What are you doing?

MARTIRIO. Nothing special.

AMELIA. What about you?

MAGDALENA. I've been running. Running through the rooms of the house. Just to go somewhere. I wanted to see those old pictures our grandmother made. You remember. The embroidery poodle and the Negro wrestling with the lion. The ones we used to love so much when we were girls. Things were better then. Weddings used to last a fortnight. And no one ever gossiped. These days everyone is so much more polite. The brides wear white veils like they do in the cities and everyone drinks wine out of bottles. But now we're all petrified in fear of what the neighbours might say and just sit here and slowly rot.

MARTIRIO. What else can we do?

AMELIA (*to* MAGDALENA). You've left your shoelace undone.

MAGDALENA. So what?

AMELIA. You'll trip and you'll fall!

MAGDALENA. One less!

MARTIRIO. Where's Adela?

MAGDALENA. Oh. She's gone and put on her green dress. The one she was going to wear on her birthday, and she's run out into the hen run and is yelling: 'Hens! Hello, hens! Look at me! Look at me!' I had to laugh!

AMELIA. If Mother catches her!

MAGDALENA. Poor soul! She is the youngest of us and still has dreams! I'd give anything to see her happy.

Pause. ANGUSTIUS *walks across the stage with some towels in her hand.*

ANGUSTIAS. What time is it?

MARTIRIO. Twelve.

ANGUSTIAS. Already?

AMELIA. It's just struck.

Exit ANGUSTIUS.

MAGDALENA (*insinuatingly, meaning* ANGUSTIUS). Have you heard…?

AMELIA. Heard what?

MAGDALENA. Go on!

MARTIRIO. We don't know what you're talking about!

MAGDALENA. I'd better tell you then. But don't tell anyone. Keep your heads together like two little sheep, and don't breathe a word! The news about Pepe el Romano!

MARTIRIO. Ah!

MAGDALENA (*mimicking her*). 'Ah!' Pepe el Romano is going to marry Angustias. People are talking about it in the village. Yesterday he was hanging about the house and today, they say, he's going to send someone round.

MARTIRIO. I'm glad. He's a good man.

AMELIA. I'm glad too. Angustias deserves him.

MAGDALENA. You're not glad at all. Neither of you are.

MARTIRIO. Magdalena!

MAGDALENA. If I thought he was really coming for her
sake, or was really attracted to her as a woman, then I
would be glad. But he's coming for the money. We all
know that. I mean, I know Angustias is our sister but
we're all family too and we can talk honestly together.
And you've got to admit that she is old and she is sickly
and looks like a stick in a dress. No. That's wrong. That's
what she looked like when she was twenty. In her prime.
Now she looks like nothing on earth.

MARTIRIO. You shouldn't say such things. Good luck
always comes to the one who least expects it.

AMELIA. No, she's right! Angustias is the only one who's
rich. It's her father's money and she gets it now because
our father is dead and they've got to divide the property.
And that's why the men are after her.

MAGDALENA. Pepe el Romano is twenty-five years old
and the best-looking man for miles around. The most
natural thing – the most human thing! – would be for him
to go after you, Amelia, or our Adela who's only twenty.
What's wrong is for him to go after the oldest, the ugliest
and the least attractive of us all. And anyway, she always
talks through her nose.

MARTIRIO. Perhaps he likes that!

MAGDALENA. I could never stand your hypocrisy!

MARTIRIO. That's not fair!

Enter ADELA.

MAGDALENA. Did the hens admire you?

ADELA. What else am I supposed to do!

AMELIA. If Mother sees you she'll scratch your eyes out!

ADELA. I love this dress. I was going to wear it the day we went to the river. We were going to sit by the watermill and eat melons, and I was going to wear it. It would be the most beautiful dress in the world.

MARTIRIO. It is lovely!

ADELA. It really suits me too. It's the best one Magdalena has ever made me.

MAGDALENA. What did the hens think of it?

ADELA. They liked it so much they gave me a present. About four million fleas to hop all over my legs!

They laugh.

MARTIRIO. The best thing to do is dye it black.

MAGDALENA. The best thing to do is give it to Angustias. She can wear it when she marries Pepe el Romano!

ADELA (*trying to hide her feelings*). But Pepe el Romano…

AMELIA. Haven't you heard?

ADELA. No.

MAGDALENA. You must have.

ADELA. It can't be true!

MAGDALENA. Anything can be true. As long as you've got the money!

ADELA. So that's why he stayed behind after the funeral.
And that's why he was looking through the bars of the
gate… (*Pause.*) And that man is capable of…

MAGDALENA. Capable of anything. Anything at all.

Pause.

MARTIRIO. What are you thinking? Adela?

ADELA. I'm thinking this is the worst time in my life for me
to have to go into mourning.

MAGDALENA. You'll get used to it.

ADELA (*bursting into tears of rage*). No, I won't get used to it! I
refuse to get used to it! I don't want to be shut up in here.
I don't want to go stale. I don't want to be like you! I don't
want my flesh to go off! I'll get up tomorrow and put on
my green dress and walk out the front door. I want out of
here! I want out!

Enter the MAID.

MAGDALENA (*sternly*). Adela!

MAID. Poor girl! How she misses her father! (*Exits.*)

MARTIRIO. Be quiet!

AMELIA. It's the same for all of us!

ADELA *calms down.*

MAGDALENA. The maid almost heard you!

MAID (*appearing*). Pepe el Romano is coming down the
street.

AMELIA, MARTIRIO *and* MAGDALENA *rush to the door.*

MAGDALENA. Let's go and see him!

Quick exit.

MAID (*to* ADELA). Aren't you going?

ADELA. No.

MAID. Once he's turned the corner you'll see him better from your room. (*Exits.*)

ADELA *stays onstage a moment, uncertain what to do. Then she quickly makes for her room. Enter* BERNARDA *and* LA PONCIA.

BERNARDA. How sordid a business this is!

LA PONCIA. The amount of money that's been left to Angustias!

BERNARDA. Yes.

LA PONCIA. And not nearly so much to the others.

BERNARDA. You've said that three times already. I didn't want to reply then, and I don't want to now. But no. Not nearly so much. A lot less. Don't remind me again.

Enter ANGUSTIUS, *with her face heavily made-up.*

Angustias!

ANGUSTIAS. Mother.

BERNARDA. How could you dare put that filth on your face? Today of all days. With your father hardly buried. How could you bear to even wash it?

ANGUSTIAS. He wasn't my father. Mine died long ago. Had you forgotten?

BERNARDA. You owe nothing to him. All he did was father you. But the man who fathered your sisters has made you a fortune!

ANGUSTIAS. That remains to be seen.

BERNARDA. Then out of decency! Out of respect!

ANGUSTIAS. Mother, can I go out now?

BERNARDA. Can you go out now? After I've taken the dirt off your face. Two-faced creature! Whore! The spitting image of your sluttish aunts!

She violently removes the make-up from ANGUSTIUS*'s face with a towel.*

Now get out!

LA PONCIA. Bernarda, you are going too far!

BERNARDA. My own mother may be mad but I have all my senses intact. I know exactly what I am doing.

Everyone comes in.

MAGDALENA. What's going on?

BERNARDA. Nothing.

MAGDALENA. If you're arguing over dividing the property, then don't worry. You're the richest and you're welcome to the lot.

ANGUSTIAS. Keep that tongue of yours locked up in its sty!

BERNARDA (*hits the floor with her stick*). Don't any of you think for a moment you're going to get the better of me! I am in command here and shall remain in command until they come to carry me out to my grave!

We hear shouts and cries and MARÍA JOSEFA,
BERNARDA's *mother, enters. She is incredibly old, garlanded
with flowers on her head and and breast.*

MARÍA JOSEFA. Where's my mantilla? Bernarda, where is
it? I don't want it to be yours. I don't want it to be
anybody's. Not my mantilla, or my rings, or my beautiful
black silk gown. None of you will ever marry. None of
you! Bernarda, give me my necklace. Give me my pearls.

BERNARDA (*to the* MAID). Why did you let her in?

MAID (*trembling*). She managed to escape!

MARÍA JOSEFA. I escaped because I want to get married. I
want to get married to a beautiful man. I'm going to get
married to a beautiful man and live by the shores of the
sea. By the sea. Not here. It's no use here. Men run away
from women here.

BERNARDA. Mother, be quiet!

MARÍA JOSEFA. No, I won't be quiet, I'm tired of these
spinster women, all desperate for men, with their hearts
slowly crumbling into dust. I don't want to see them any
more. I want to go back to my village, Bernarda, back to
where I belong. I want a man to marry and be happy!

BERNARDA. Lock her up!

MARÍA JOSEFA. Don't lock me up, Bernarda! Don't lock
me up! Let me go!

The MAID *seizes* MARÍA JOSEFA.

BERNARDA. Help her, all of you!

They all drag MARÍA JOSEFA *away.*

MARÍA JOSEFA. Let me go! Let me go! Bernarda! I want to get married! By the shores of the sea, by the shores of the sea!

Quick curtain.

End of Act One.

ACT TWO

White room inside BERNARDA's *house. Doors to the left lead to the bedrooms.* BERNARDA's DAUGHTERS *are sitting in chairs, sewing.* MAGDALENA *embroiders.* LA PONCIA *is with them.*

ANGUSTIAS. I've just finished the third sheet.

MARTIRIO. For the third daughter. Amelia: your sheet.

MAGDALENA. What shall I put on yours, Angustias? Shall I put on Pepe's initials too?

ANGUSTIAS (*curtly*). No.

MAGDALENA (*loudly*). Adela, are you coming?

AMELIA. She'll be in bed.

LA PONCIA. There's something wrong with that girl. She's always trembling. She's frightened of something. And she won't keep still. As if she had a lizard between her breasts.

MARTIRIO. She's just like the rest of us. She's got to put up with it.

MAGDALENA. All of us except Angustias.

ANGUSTIAS. And I'm fine, thank you very much, and anyone who doesn't like it will just have to explode.

MAGDALENA. You've always been noted for your tact.

ANGUSTIAS. Fortunately I am about to leave this hell.

MAGDALENA. Let's hope you never do.

MARTIRIO. That's enough, both of you!

ANGUSTIAS. Better to have gold in your chest than pretty eyes in your face!

MAGDALENA. It's all just going in one ear and out the other.

AMELIA (*to* LA PONCIA). Open the door a bit and let in some fresh air.

LA PONCIA *does so.*

MARTIRIO. Last night I was so hot I couldn't sleep a wink.

AMELIA. Me neither!

MARTIRIO. I had to get up to try and cool down. There was this great dark storm cloud in the sky and I could have sworn I felt a few drops of rain.

LA PONCIA. It was one in the morning. The earth breathed fire. I got up too. Angustias was still at the window with Pepe.

MAGDALENA (*ironically*). So late? What time did he go?

ANGUSTIAS. Why ask if you saw him yourself?

AMELIA. He must have left about half-past one.

ANGUSTIAS. How do you know?

AMELIA. I heard him cough and I heard the hooves of his mare.

LA PONCIA. But I heard him about four!

ANGUSTIAS. You can't have done.

LA PONCIA. I'm sure I did!

MARTIRIO. I thought I heard something too.

MAGDALENA. How very strange!

Pause.

LA PONCIA. Angustias, tell us what he said. Go on. What did he say the first time he came to your window?

ANGUSTIAS. Nothing special. What do you think he'd say? He just said… ordinary things. Things people say.

MARTIRIO. It really is the oddest thing. I mean, there's two people who don't know each other at all. Who've never even spoken to each other in their lives before. And suddenly there they are. At a window. Looking at each other through iron bars. About to get married.

ANGUSTIAS. But that's the way it's done. It's just normal. It doesn't feel a bit strange to me.

AMELIA. It would make me feel funny.

ANGUSTIAS. But it doesn't. Not when it happens. Because when a man comes up to you at the window it's all been settled already. He knows you've got to say yes.

MARTIRIO. Yes, but he's still got to ask.

ANGUSTIAS. Obviously!

AMELIA (*with avid curiosity*). Then what did he say?

ANGUSTIAS. He just said, 'You know I want you. I need a woman who's good, and well-behaved, and if you agree, that's you.'

AMELIA. Things like that make me feel ashamed!

ANGUSTIAS. Me too, but you just have to put up with them!

LA PONCIA. Is that all?

ANGUSTIAS. He said other things too. He did all the talking.

MARTIRIO. But what about you?

ANGUSTIAS. I couldn't say a word. I was too frightened. It was the first time I'd ever been alone with a man.

MAGDALENA. And such a handsome man too.

ANGUSTIAS. He's quite good-looking!

LA PONCIA. The things that happen when people start to know what they're doing! The things they say and do with their hands…! The first time my husband Evaristo el Colorín came to my window… (*Laughs.*)

AMELIA. What happened?

LA PONCIA. It was really dark. But I could see him coming. And when he got up to the window, he said, 'Good evening.' And then I said, 'Good evening,' and then we never said a word for half an hour. I was drenched in sweat. And then Evaristo came up to me, came up so close it was as if he wanted to squeeze between the bars and he said, in a very low voice, he said, 'Come here so I can feel you!'

They all laugh. AMELIA suddenly breaks off and runs to listen at a door.

AMELIA. Oh! I thought I could hear Mother coming.

MAGDALENA. She'd have skinned us alive!

They keep on laughing.

AMELIA. Ssssshhhh! She's going to hear us!

LA PONCIA. After that he behaved himself. He could have taken up all sorts of things, but instead he took up canaries. None of you are married, and when you are, the first thing you've got to learn is that after a fortnight your man'll get tired of making love. All he'll care about then is his stomach. And after a fortnight of that, all he'll care about is the nearest bar. And anyone who doesn't like it just has to go inside a corner and cry herself to pieces.

AMELIA. You didn't do that.

LA PONCIA. I could stand up to him!

MARTIRIO. Is it true you used to beat him?

LA PONCIA. Of course. I tell you, once I almost poked his eye out.

MAGDALENA. That's the way women should be!

LA PONCIA. I'm like your mother. One day he said something that really annoyed me and I killed all his canaries. I took the pestle and squashed their heads. It was something he said. Really got up my nose. I can't remember what it was now.

They all laugh.

MAGDALENA. Adela, don't miss this.

AMELIA. Adela.

Pause.

MAGDALENA. I'll go and see! (*Goes into her room.*)

LA PONCIA. That girl's ill!

MARTIRIO. What else do you expect? She hardly ever sleeps!

LA PONCIA. Then what does she do at night?

MARTIRIO. Do you really want to know?

LA PONCIA. You'll know better than me. You sleep next door.

ANGUSTIAS. She's eaten up by envy.

AMELIA. Don't exaggerate.

ANGUSTIAS. No, it's true. I can see it in her eyes. She's starting to look a bit mad.

MARTIRIO. Don't talk about madness. Not here. Don't even mention the word!

Enter MAGDALENA *with* ADELA.

MAGDALENA. I thought you'd have been asleep.

ADELA. I couldn't sleep. My body's gone bad.

MARTIRIO (*pointedly*). You don't get enough sleep at night.

ADELA. Maybe.

MARTIRIO. Well then?

ADELA (*fiercely*). Leave me alone! It's none of your business how much I sleep! What I do with my body is up to me!

MARTIRIO. We're just worried about you!

ADELA. Worried, were you? You're just nosey! Weren't you sewing? Well, get on with it. Sew! I wish I was invisible, so I could walk through this house without anyone asking me where I was going!

MAID (*entering*). Bernarda wants you. The man's come with the lace.

They exit. As she goes, MARTIRIO *stares at* ADELA.

ADELA. Don't look at me! With your dead eyes. Have mine if you like. They still shine. Or have my shoulders to straighten the crook in your back, only don't keep looking at me! Just don't look at me!

Exit MARTIRIO.

LA PONCIA. Adela, she's your sister. She's the one who loves you most!

ADELA. She follows me about everywhere. Sometimes she pokes her nose into my room to see if I'm asleep. She doesn't let me breathe. And she goes on about me all the time. All about my face, which will go old, and my body, which will go to waste. And she's wrong. She's wrong! I'll give my body to whoever I please!

LA PONCIA (*pointedly, in a low voice*). To Pepe, Adela?

ADELA (*startled*). What did you say?

LA PONCIA. You heard me!

ADELA. Be quiet!

LA PONCIA (*loudly*). Did you think I hadn't noticed?

ADELA. Keep your voice down!

LA PONCIA. Kill these dreams!

ADELA. How much do you know?

LA PONCIA. Where do you go when you get up at night?
We can see you. See you go. We old women can see
through walls.

ADELA. I wish you were blind!

LA PONCIA. I have twenty pairs of eyes. Eyes in my hands.
Eyes in my feet. Eyes everywhere when I need them. And
I need them now. Need them to keep track of what you
and Pepe are up to. Though for the life of me I don't
understand what you think you'll get from him just now.
Why did you stand at the window the last time Pepe
came? Why did you open the window and turn on the
light? Why did you take off your clothes?

ADELA. It's not true!

LA PONCIA. Don't be like a baby! Leave your sister alone,
and if you fancy Pepe then it's just too bad. You'll have to
put up with it.

ADELA *cries.*

And anyway, who says you can't marry him? Your sister
Angustias is an invalid. She won't survive her first child.
She's old and sickly and she's got narrow hips and I can
tell you she'll die. I know. Then Pepe will do what all
widowers do round here: he'll marry the youngest and
most beautiful sister. And that's you. Feed on that hope,
and forget the rest. But don't break the law of God.

ADELA. Be quiet!

LA PONCIA. I won't be quiet!

ADELA. Mind your own business. Stop snooping!

LA PONCIA. I'll be closer to you than your own shadow!

ADELA. Why don't you just clean the house? Why don't you
    just go to bed at night and pray over all your dead bodies?
    Why do you have to stick your nose into other people's
    affairs? Snuffling about in the dirt like a sow!

LA PONCIA. I keep alert! I don't want people to spit as they
    pass this door.

ADELA. What's made you suddenly so fond of my sister?

LA PONCIA. I don't care about her at all. Not about her,
    not about any of you. I just don't want to live in a house
    of ill repute. I'm too old to get involved in dirt!

ADELA. It's too late. Anything you say is useless. I'll push
    you in the dirt and walk right over you. And I'll do the
    same to my mother. Anything to quench this fire that
    burns between my legs and in my mouth. But you've got
    nothing on me. What can you say against me? That I lock
    myself in my room and won't open the door? Nothing
    wrong with that! That I don't sleep? I'm not the only one!
    I'm cleverer than you! You'll see. I'm quick as a hare.
    Quicker! Just you see! I'll slip between your fingers!

LA PONCIA. Don't challenge me. Adela, don't challenge
    me! Nothing escapes me. Keep something dark, and I'll
    bring it to light! Hush something up, and I'll shout it out
    loud! I can set the bells ringing!

ADELA. Even if you took four thousand yellow flares and lit
    them in every corner of the yard, you still couldn't stop
    me. No one can. It has to happen, Poncia. Has to. No one
    can stop it.

LA PONCIA. You love him that much!

ADELA. That much! When I look into his eyes I feel like I'm drinking his blood. Drop by drop by drop!

LA PONCIA. I won't hear this!

ADELA. You'll hear it! I used to be scared of you. But no more. Now I am stronger than you!

Enter ANGUSTIUS.

ANGUSTIAS. Still talking!

LA PONCIA. She keeps insisting I go out in this heat and buy her some piece of nonsense from the shop.

ANGUSTIAS. Did you get me the perfume?

LA PONCIA. Yes. The most expensive in the shop. And the powder. I've put them on the table in your room.

Exit ANGUSTIUS.

ADELA. And hush!

LA PONCIA. We'll see!

Enter MARTIRIO, *carrying some pieces of lace,* AMELIA, *and* MAGDALENA.

MAGDALENA (*to* ADELA). Have you seen the lace?

AMELIA. Those pieces Angustias bought for her wedding sheets are just beautiful.

ADELA (*to* MARTIRIO). What are those for?

MARTIRIO. They're for me. For a petticoat.

ADELA (*sarcastically*). We all have our dreams!

MARTIRIO (*pointedly*). They're just for me. No one else. I don't need to display myself.

LA PONCIA. No one ever sees your petticoat.

MARTIRIO (*pointedly, looking at* ADELA). Sometimes people do! Besides, I love underwear. If I was rich, I'd have it all in silk. It's one of the few things I can still enjoy.

LA PONCIA. This kind of lace looks lovely on a baby's bonnet. Or a christening robe. I could never afford it for mine. I wonder if Angustias will use it for hers. She'll keep you sewing night and day if she takes it into her head to breed.

MAGDALENA. I don't intend to sew a single stitch. Not for her.

AMELIA. And I'm not going to look after anyone else's kids. Look at those people in the alley, run off their feet for four brats.

LA PONCIA. They're still better off than you. Things happen in their house. People hit each other. People laugh!

MARTIRIO. So why don't you work for them?

LA PONCIA. Because I'm stuck here, that's why. Stuck with this convent.

We hear little bells in the distance, as if through various walls.

MAGDALENA. It's the men going back to work.

MARTIRIO. In this sun!

LA PONCIA. It struck three a minute ago.

ADELA (*sitting down*). Oh, I wish I could go out to the fields!

MAGDALENA (*sitting down*). Each according to their class!

MARTIRIO (*sitting down*). That's how it is!

AMELIA (*sitting down*). Worse luck!

LA PONCIA. This time of year there is nowhere like the fields. Nowhere better. Yesterday morning the reapers came. Forty young men. Forty handsome young men.

MAGDALENA. Where have they come from?

LA PONCIA. Far away. From the mountains. They're full of joy! They sing and throw stones! And yesterday a woman came. She had sequins all over her dress and she danced to a tambourine. Twenty of them made a deal with her and took her to the olive grove. I watched them. The boy who hired her was firm and strong and had green eyes.

AMELIA. Is that true?

ADELA. It could be!

LA PONCIA. Years ago another came and I gave my son money to go with her. Men need these things.

ADELA. They're forgiven everything.

AMELIA. If you're a woman, you're punished just by being born.

MAGDALENA. We don't even own our eyes!

We hear a distant song getting closer and closer.

LA PONCIA. It's them. Singing. They have wonderful songs.

AMELIA. They are going out to reap.

SONG. The reapers go out in the fields,
    Searching for the ears of the wheat,
    What they find are the hearts of the girls,
    Who fall in love with them when they meet.

We hear tambouines and drums. Pause. All listen in total silence, a silence pierced through and through by the heat.

AMELIA. Don't they care about the heat!

MARTIRIO. It licks them with tongues of fire.

ADELA. I'd like to be a reaper. To be free to come and go. To forget this longing.

MARTIRIO. What longing have you to forget?

ADELA. Everyone has something.

MARTIRIO (*with deep meaning*). Everyone.

LA PONCIA. Quiet! Quiet!

SONG (*very far away*). There's a girl behind each window,
    A girl behind each door,
    Open them and hand out roses,
    The reaper wants some more…

LA PONCIA. What a beautiful song!

MARTIRIO (*nostalgically*). There's a girl behind each window,
    A girl behind each door…

ADELA (*passionately*). Open them and hand out roses,
    The reaper wants some more…

The sound goes further and further and further away.

LA PONCIA. Now they're turning the corner.

ADELA. Let's watch them from my room.

LA PONCIA. Don't open the window. Open it just a crack and they'll push it open wide.

LA PONCIA, MAGDALENA *and* ADELA *go off.* MARTIRIO *stays behind. She remains sitting in a low seat with her head between her hands.*

AMELIA (*coming up to her*). What's wrong?

MARTIRIO. I can't stand the heat.

AMELIA. Is that really all?

MARTIRIO. I wish the rain would come. I wish it was November. I can't wait for the frosts. Anything except this endless summer.

AMELIA. It'll all pass and then come back again.

MARTIRIO. I know! (*Pause.*) What time did you get to sleep last night?

AMELIA. I don't know. I sleep like a log. Why?

MARTIRIO. No reason, I just thought I heard people in the yard.

AMELIA. Did you?

MARTIRIO. Very late.

AMELIA. Weren't you frightened?

MARTIRIO. No. I've heard it before.

AMELIA. We should be careful. Couldn't it have been the farmhands?

MARTIRIO. They don't come till six.

AMELIA. Perhaps it was the young mule that hasn't been broken in yet.

MARTIRIO (*through gritted teeth and with heavy irony*). That'll be right. The young mule that hasn't been broken in yet!

AMELIA. We should tell someone!

MARTIRIO. No! Not yet! Don't mention it to anybody! I could have just imagined it.

AMELIA. Maybe.

Pause. AMELIA starts to go off.

MARTIRIO. Amelia.

AMELIA (*at the door*). What?

Pause.

MARTIRIO. Nothing.

Pause.

AMELIA. Why did you call me?

Pause.

MARTIRIO. I don't know. I just did. I'd said it before I realised.

Pause.

AMELIA. You should go and lie down.

ANGUSTIUS *comes onstage furiously, so there is a great contrast between this scene and the previous silences.*

ANGUSTIAS. Where's the picture of Pepe I keep under my pillow? Who's taken it?

MARTIRIO. Not me.

AMELIA. Nor me. I'd never take it. Not even if he were a pin-up saint in silver. Which he isn't.

Enter LA PONCIA, MAGDALENA *and* ADELA.

ANGUSTIAS. Where's my picture?

ADELA. What picture?

ANGUSTIAS. The one you've taken from me.

MAGDALENA. You've got a nerve to say that!

ANGUSTIAS. It was in my room yesterday and it's not there now.

MARTIRIO. I expect it got up last night and went for a walk in the yard. Pepe loves the fresh air.

ANGUSTIAS. That's not funny! When I find it I'll tell Mother.

LA PONCIA. Don't tell anyone! I'm sure it'll turn up! (*Looking at* ADELA.)

ANGUSTIAS. I'd like to know which one of you has got it!

ADELA (*looking at* MARTIRIO). Someone's got it, I wonder who!

MARTIRIO (*ironically*). I wonder!

BERNARDA (*coming in with her stick*). What is the meaning of this scandalous noise? In this heat there should be nothing but silence! All the neighbours will have their ears glued to the walls!

ANGUSTIAS. Someone's taken my fiancé's picture.

BERNARDA (*fiercely*). Who was it? Who?

ANGUSTIAS. One of them!

BERNARDA. Which one? (*Silence.*) Answer me! (*Silence. To* LA PONCIA.) Search all their rooms. Look under their beds. This is what comes of my being so slack! But don't think you can get away from me. I'll come back to haunt you in your dreams! (*To* ANGUSTIUS.) Are you sure you didn't lose it?

ANGUSTIAS. Certain.

BERNARDA. You've had a good look for it?

ANGUSTIAS. Yes, Mother.

Everyone is standing in a painful silence.

BERNARDA. And now at the end of my life you give me this bitter pill to swallow. The most vicious blow a mother has ever had to endure. (*To* LA PONCIA.) Haven't you found it yet?

Enter LA PONCIA.

LA PONCIA. Here it is.

BERNARDA. Where did you find it?

LA PONCIA. It was…

BERNARDA. Don't be afraid to say.

LA PONCIA (*surprised*). It was between the sheets of Martirio's bed.

BERNARDA (*to* MARTIRIO). Is that true?

MARTIRIO. Yes. It's true!

BERNARDA (*going up to* MARTIRIO *and hitting her with the stick*). Insect! Despicable little thief! I'd like to squash you flat and wipe you off the soles of my feet! Little wretch!

MARTIRIO (*fiercely*). Mother, don't hit me!

BERNARDA. I'll hit you as much as I like!

MARTIRIO. Only because I let you. Now stop! Do you hear me?

LA PONCIA. Show more respect to your mother!

ANGUSTIAS (*grabbing* BERNARDA). Leave her. Please!

BERNARDA. There's not a single tear in her eyes.

MARTIRIO. I won't cry just to give you pleasure.

BERNARDA. Why did you take the picture?

MARTIRIO. Can't I play a joke on my own sister? What else should I want it for?

ADELA (*exploding with jealousy*). That was no joke. You've never played a joke on anybody. You had something very different in mind. Admit it. Something is burning you up. Admit it!

MARTIRIO. Keep your mouth shut and don't dare make me speak. Because if I do I'll tell something that'll make even the walls hide their heads in shame.

ADELA. There's something about malicious people. They just can't stop telling lies.

BERNARDA. Adela!

MAGDALENA. You've both gone mad.

AMELIA. You're infecting us with evil thoughts.

MARTIRIO. Others do worse.

ADELA. Until they go too far. Then they're stripped naked for the world to see and the river sweeps them away.

BERNARDA. Shameless girl!

ANGUSTIAS. I can't help it if Pepe el Romano finds me attractive.

ADELA. Not you. Your money!

ANGUSTIAS. Mother!

BERNARDA. Silence!

MARTIRIO. Your fields and olive trees.

MAGDALENA. They're right!

BERNARDA. I said silence! I could see this storm coming, but I didn't think that it would break so soon. What a hail storm of hatred you've made break on my heart! But I'm not finished yet. I'll forge five chains of steel to bind you tight. I'll bolt and I'll bar every door against you, every door in my father's house so not even the walls will know my shame! Now get out, all of you! Get out!

The DAUGHTERS *leave.* BERNARDA *sits down, desolate.*
LA PONCIA *is standing, leaning against a wall.*
BERNARDA *suddenly strikes the floor with her stick and says:*

I will have to make them feel the weight of my hand! That is your duty, Bernarda. Your duty. And don't you forget it.

LA PONCIA. May I speak?

BERNARDA. Speak. I am sorry you heard. A stranger should never be allowed into a family's heart.

LA PONCIA. It can't be helped. I have seen what I have seen.

BERNARDA. Angustias must marry at once.

LA PONCIA. Obviously, you have to get her out of here.

BERNARDA. Not her. Him!

LA PONCIA. Him, yes. Obviously. You have to get him out of here! You're right to think that.

BERNARDA. I don't think. There are some things that cannot and should not be thought. I order.

LA PONCIA. And do you think he'll want to go?

BERNARDA (*standing up*). What's going on in that head of yours?

LA PONCIA. Nothing. He'll marry Angustias. Obviously.

BERNARDA. You've got something vicious hidden up your sleeve. I can tell. I know you too well. You can't wait to stick the knife in. Speak.

LA PONCIA. I don't want to stick the knife in. I just want to help. Helping and murdering aren't quite the same thing. I'm surprised you haven't noticed.

BERNARDA. Are you trying to warn me of something?

LA PONCIA. I don't blame you, Bernarda. I'm not accusing anyone. All I'm saying is this: look about you. Open your eyes.

BERNARDA. And what do you think I'll see?

LA PONCIA. You've always kept your eyes open. You've been able to see other people's faults from miles off. I've often thought you could read people's minds. But now you've gone blind. All of a sudden. Still, I suppose one's own family is something else altogether.

BERNARDA. Are you talking about Martirio?

LA PONCIA. Yes, if you like, Martirio… (*Curiously.*) Why should she have wanted to hide the picture?

BERNARDA (*wanting to make excuses for her daughter*). She said herself it was just a joke. What else could it have been?

LA PONCIA (*sarcastically*). You really think so?

BERNARDA (*vehemently*). I don't think so. I know!

LA PONCIA. That'll be right then. It's your family. You know best. But would it still be a joke if it was one of the neighbours?

BERNARDA. Now you're starting to stick the knife in.

LA PONCIA (*still with a cruel edge to her voice*). No, Bernarda. I wouldn't want to do that. It's just that something very big is happening here. I don't want to blame you for it, but you've never given your daughters any freedom at all. You can say what you like, but Martirio… is just desperate to fall in love. With anybody. Why didn't you let her marry Enrique Humanes? Why was it that the very day he was going to see her you sent him a message forbidding him to come?

BERNARDA (*fiercely*). And if I had to I'd do it again! And again and again! No one in my family marries the Humanes while I've got breath in my body! His father was a common labourer.

LA PONCIA. You and your airs!

BERNARDA. If I have airs it's because I've a right to them. And if you don't it's because of where you sprang from.

LA PONCIA (*with hatred*). Don't remind me! I'm too old for that. And I've always been grateful for your support.

BERNARDA (*pompously*). It doesn't sound like it!

LA PONCIA (*with her hatred hidden in gentleness*). Martirio will get over this.

BERNARDA. And if she doesn't, so much the worse for her! I don't think that is the 'very big thing' that is going on here. According to you. Nothing is going on here. And if anything did ever 'go on', you can be sure that word of it would never go beyond these walls.

LA PONCIA. I wouldn't be so sure! Other people in the village can also read people's minds. You're not the only one.

BERNARDA. How you'd love to see me and my daughters on the road to the brothel!

LA PONCIA. No one can predict where they might end up!

BERNARDA. I know where I'll end up! And my daughters! The brothel is the place for a certain woman who's already dead…

LA PONCIA (*fiercely*). Bernarda, have respect for my mother's memory!

BERNARDA. Then don't torment me with your wicked thoughts!

Pause.

LA PONCIA. I'd be better not getting involved.

BERNARDA. Exactly. Don't get involved. Keep your mouth shut. Do your work. That is the duty of the employee.

LA PONCIA. But I can't. I mean... don't you think that Pepe would be better married to Martirio, or even – better still! – to Adela?

BERNARDA. No.

LA PONCIA (*deliberately*). Adela. Now there's the proper wife for Pepe!

BERNARDA. Things never work out the way we'd like them to.

LA PONCIA. But it's hard to twist them from their proper course. I think it's wrong for Pepe to marry Angustias, and I'm not the only one. Other people think so too. It's in the air. And who knows what it may lead to in the end!

BERNARDA. There you go again! You're going out of your way to fill my mind with nightmares. I'm not going to listen to you, which is just as well. Because if I did, and if I really came to fully understand everything you are hinting at, I'd have to scratch out your eyes.

LA PONCIA. I wouldn't let you get near them!

BERNARDA. Fortunately I have my daughters' respect. And I have always had their obedience!

LA PONCIA. Oh yes, their obedience! Release them from that, and they'd be flying over the rooftops!

BERNARDA. I'd climb up myself and bring them down with grappling irons.

LA PONCIA. You were always strong!

BERNARDA. I can take care of myself!

LA PONCIA. But how things have changed! Even at her age, you should see how keen Angustias is over her man! He seems dead keen too! My eldest son told me that as he was going by with his oxen at dawn, they were still at it together. At four in the morning!

BERNARDA. At four in the morning!

ANGUSTIAS (*entering*). It's a lie!

LA PONCIA. That's what my son told me.

BERNARDA. Tell me the truth!

ANGUSTIAS. For more than a week now, Pepe has been leaving at one. God kill me if I lie.

MARTIRIO (*entering*). I also heard him leave at four.

BERNARDA. But – did you see him?

MARTIRIO. I didn't want to lean out of the window. Don't you meet now at the window that gives onto the alleyway?

ANGUSTIAS. He comes to my bedroom window.

ADELA *appears at her door.*

MARTIRIO. Then…

BERNARDA. What are you hinting at?

LA PONCIA. If you find out, you'll regret it! One thing's for sure: that Pepe was talking to someone at four in the morning. Someone who lives in your house.

BERNARDA. Do you know that for sure?

LA PONCIA. In this life, one can't ever be sure.

ADELA. Mother, don't you listen to someone who just wants to defame us all.

BERNARDA. I'll find out what I need to! And if people in the village want to throw slanders at me, I'll stand there like flint and dash them to pieces! We won't talk of this again. Sometimes people want to dig a pit of filth and push us into it to drown there.

MARTIRIO. I don't like to tell lies.

LA PONCIA. There must be something to it.

BERNARDA. There's nothing in it! I was born with my eyes wide open! Now I'll never shut them till the day I die.

ANGUSTIAS. But I've got a right to find out the truth.

BERNARDA. You've a right to nothing but obedience! And I'll have no one giving the orders here but me! (*To* LA PONCIA.) And you just stick to your job. And remember, all of you: I'm watching every step you take. Every little thing you do, I'll know all about it.

MAID (*entering*). There's a great crowd at the top of the street and all the neighbours are at their doors!

BERNARDA (*to* LA PONCIA). Run and find out what's going on!

Everyone starts to make for the door.

And where do you think you're going? I might have known you'd be the kind of women to hang about at windows and have no respect for their dead! Get back inside!

They exit, and so does BERNARDA. *We can hear distant shouts.
Enter* ADELA *and* MARTIRIO, *who stay for a moment
listening, without daring to take another step towards the front door.*

MARTIRIO. You're lucky I didn't talk!

ADELA. I could have spoken too.

MARTIRIO. And what could you have said? I've done
nothing!

ADELA. Just because you haven't dared to. It takes guts to
get anything done, and you haven't got it in you. No, you
haven't done anything. You've just wanted to.

MARTIRIO. You can't go on like this for long.

ADELA. I'll have him all to myself!

MARTIRIO. I'll break it up.

ADELA (*pleading*). Martirio, let me be!

MARTIRIO. Never!

ADELA. He wants me to live with him!

MARTIRIO. I've watched him kiss you!

ADELA. I didn't want to. Not at first! I just felt tied to him.
At the end of a chain! And he just dragged me towards
him. I couldn't help it!

MARTIRIO. You'd be better off dead!

MAGDALENA *and* ANGUSTIUS *poke their heads round
their doors. We can hear the tumult rising.*

LA PONCIA (*entering with* BERNARDA). Bernarda!

BERNARDA. What's happening?

LA PONCIA. La Librada's unmarried daughter had a son and no one knows its father.

ADELA. She had a son?

LA PONCIA. And she killed it to hide her shame. She buried it under some stones. The dogs found it. It was as if they had more heart than her. They pulled it out and God guided them to her door. That's where they left it. On her threshold. Now everyone wants to kill her. They're dragging her down the street, and the men are coming running through the fields, shouting so loud they're shaking the trees.

BERNARDA. Good. Let them come. Let them come with sticks and with heavy stones and beat her to death.

ADELA. They mustn't kill her. They mustn't.

MARTIRIO. Oh, but they must. Let's go out to watch.

BERNARDA. Let her pay the penalty for her shame.

We hear a woman scream outside. The tumult grows.

ADELA. Let her go free! Don't go outside!

MARTIRIO (*looking at* ADELA). Let her pay for what she's done!

BERNARDA (*at the front door*). Kill her before the police come! Heap her with burning coals in the place of her sin!

ADELA (*clutching her belly*). No! No!

BERNARDA. Kill her! Kill her!

Curtain.

End of Act Two.

ACT THREE

The inner courtyard of BERNARDA's *house. The walls are white with a hint of blue. It is night-time. The decor needs to be utterly simple. The doorways are lit from the rooms within and give the stage a feeble glow of light.*

In the centre is a table lit by an oil lamp, where BERNARDA *and her* DAUGHTERS *are eating.* LA PONCIA *serves them.* PRUDENCIA *is sitting on her own.*

The curtain rises in the midst of profound silence, broken only by the clatter of crockery and the sounds of knives and forks.

PRUDENCIA. I must go, I've been here far too long.

BERNARDA. Don't go. We hardly ever see each other.

PRUDENCIA. Have they rung for the last rosary?

LA PONCIA. Not yet.

    PRUDENCIA *sits down.*

BERNARDA. And how's your husband?

PRUDENCIA. The same.

BERNARDA. We never see him, either.

PRUDENCIA. You know how he is. Ever since he quarrelled with his brothers over the inheritance, he's never been out the front door. He takes a ladder and climbs out over the walls.

BERNARDA. There's a real man for you. And how is he with your daughter?

PRUDENCIA. He has never forgiven her.

BERNARDA. Quite right. She is an enemy now. A daughter who disobeys is a daughter no more.

PRUDENCIA. I'd rather let things be. My only consolation is to go to church. But I'll have to stop going now. My sight's fading, and the boys are beginning to torment me. So hateful to be the sport of urchins.

We hear a heavy blow, as if something is striking the walls.

What was that?

BERNARDA. The stallion. He must be kicking the wall. We locked him up in the stable. He'll be feeling the heat. (*Shouts.*) Hobble it and let it out in the yard!

PRUDENCIA. Will you give him the new fillies?

BERNARDA. At dawn.

PRUDENCIA. And your herd's so big already. You've done terribly well.

BERNARDA. I've worked and suffered for it.

LA PONCIA (*butting in*). She's got the best stock for miles around! Pity the price has fallen.

BERNARDA. Would you like some cheese and honey?

PRUDENCIA. I have no appetite.

We hear the blow again.

LA PONCIA. For the love of God!

PRUDENCIA. It gave me such a fright! It sent shivers up my spine.

BERNARDA (*getting up angrily*). Have I got to tell you everything twice? Let him out so he can roll in the hay! (*Pause. As if speaking to the labourers.*) Then shut the fillies in the stable! But let him go free. Or else he'll kick the walls down. (*Goes back to the table and sits down again.*) What a life!

LA PONCIA. Toiling away like a man.

BERNARDA. That's how it is.

ADELA *gets up from the table.*

Where are you going?

ADELA. To get a drink of water.

BERNARDA (*loudly*). Bring a jug of cool water. (*To* ADELA.) You can sit down now.

ADELA *sits down.*

PRUDENCIA. And when will Angustias be married?

BERNARDA. His family are coming to arrange it in three days.

PRUDENCIA. You must be so happy!

ANGUSTIAS. Yes!

AMELIA (*to* MAGDALENA). Now you've spilt the salt!

MAGDALENA. Your luck can hardly get any worse. It's bad enough already.

AMELIA. It's still a bad sign.

BERNARDA. Nonsense!

PRUDENCIA (*to* ANGUSTIUS). Has he given you a ring?

ANGUSTIAS. Yes. Look. (*Shows it.*)

PRUDENCIA. Pearls. How lovely. But in my day, pearls meant tears.

ANGUSTIAS. But now things have changed.

ADELA. I don't agree. Things don't change their meaning. Engagement rings should be made of diamonds.

PRUDENCIA. That would be more proper.

BERNARDA. Pearls or diamonds, it's all the same. It doesn't matter. What matters is that things turn out the way one intends.

MARTIRIO. Or the way God ordains them.

PRUDENCIA. They tell me the furniture is beautiful.

BERNARDA. It should be. It cost me sixteen thousand reales.

LA PONCIA. I'll tell you what's best of all. The wardrobe. It's got a full-length mirror.

PRUDENCIA. I've never seen a wardrobe.

BERNARDA. In my day we used a chest.

PRUDENCIA. The main thing is for everything to turn out well.

ADELA. And that is something no one can predict.

BERNARDA. There is no reason to imagine otherwise.

We hear bells ringing a long, long way off.

PRUDENCIA. The last bell. (*To* ANGUSTIUS.) I must come back so you can show me your dress.

ANGUSTIAS. Whenever you wish.

PRUDENCIA. God give us all a good night's rest.

BERNARDA. Goodbye, Prudencia.

THE FIVE DAUGHTERS (*together*). May you go with God.

Pause. Exit PRUDENCIA.

BERNARDA. The meal is over.

All stand up.

ADELA. I'm going to the yard to stretch my legs and get a breath of fresh air.

MAGDALENA *sits on a low seat, leaning against the wall.*

AMELIA. Me too.

MARTIRIO. And me.

ADELA (*with suppressed hatred*). I'm hardly likely to get lost.

AMELIA. At night it's best not to be alone.

They exit. BERNARDA *sits down and* ANGUSTIUS *clears the table.*

BERNARDA. You must make it up with your sister. I've told you once already. I don't want to have to tell you again. What happened over the picture was a joke and you should forget all about it.

AMELIA. Martirio doesn't love me.

BERNARDA. I'm not concerned with feelings. What people feel is their own affair. What matters is the way things look. Harmony in the family. That's what concerns me. Do I make myself clear?

ANGUSTIAS. Yes, Mother.

BERNARDA. Then there's nothing else to be said.

MAGDALENA (*half-asleep*). Anyway, you'll soon be gone.

She sleeps.

ANGUSTIAS. Not soon enough for me.

BERNARDA. What time did you and Pepe finish last night?

ANGUSTIAS. Half-past twelve.

BERNARDA. And what does Pepe have to say for himself?

ANGUSTIAS. I don't know. He's always so distracted. He always seems to be thinking of something else and when I ask him what's on his mind, he just says, 'Men's affairs.'

BERNARDA. You should never have asked. Not now, and certainly not when you're married. Don't look at him unless he looks at you first. And speak only when you're spoken to. That way you'll have no trouble.

ANGUSTIAS. I think he's hiding something from me.

BERNARDA. Don't try to find out what it is. Never ask him. Above all, never let him see you cry.

ANGUSTIAS. I know I should feel happy, but I just feel wretched.

BERNARDA. If you should be happy then you are happy. They are one and the same.

ANGUSTIAS. I want to know him better. I look at him as hard as I can but he just gets all blurred. And all I see through the bars of my window is this shadow who seems shrouded in dust.

BERNARDA. That's just weakness. You'll get over it.

ANGUSTIAS. I hope so!

BERNARDA. Is he coming tonight?

ANGUSTIAS. No. He said he and his mother were going to town.

BERNARDA. Good. We'll all get an early night. Magdalena!

ANGUSTIAS. She's fast asleep.

Enter ADELA, MARTIRIO *and* AMELIA.

AMELIA. How dark it is out there!

ADELA. You can hardly see two paces in front of you.

MARTIRIO. A good night for robbers. And for liars.

ADELA. The stallion was standing in the middle of the yard. He was so white! He seemed to fill the darkness.

AMELIA. I was frightened. It looked like a ghost.

ADELA. There are stars in the sky as big as my fist.

MARTIRIO. She was staring at them so hard she almost cricked her neck. If she'd stared at them much more, her head would have snapped off.

ADELA. Don't you like the stars?

MARTIRIO. No. I don't care for them at all. Why should I? There's enough going on inside.

ADELA. That just about sums you up.

BERNARDA. You see things one way; she sees them another. She's got a right to.

ANGUSTIAS. Goodnight.

ADELA. Off to bed already?

ANGUSTIAS. Yes. Pepe is not coming tonight. (*Exits.*)

ADELA. Mother, why is it that whenever people see a flash of lightning or a shooting star they say 'God bless St Barbara, God's writing in the sky'?

BERNARDA. In the old days people knew things that have now been forgotten.

AMELIA. I hate shooting stars. I don't want to see them. I'd rather close my eyes.

ADELA. I love them. Just think of it: a desolate patch of sky, where everything's been quiet and dead for millions and millions of years and then suddenly – phweeeee! A shooting star.

MARTIRIO. But that's got nothing to do with us.

BERNARDA. So it's better not to think of it.

ADELA. It's so beautiful tonight. And the air is fresh and cool. I'd like to stay up all night to enjoy it.

BERNARDA. It's time we were all in bed. Magdalena!

AMELIA. Still fast asleep.

BERNARDA. Magdalena!

MAGDALENA (*crossly*). Leave me alone!

BERNARDA. Go to bed!

MAGDALENA (*getting up bad-temperedly*). Can't a body get a moment's peace? (*Goes off grumbling.*)

AMELIA. Goodnight. (*Exits.*)

BERNARDA. And you go too.

MARTIRIO. Why isn't Pepe coming?

BERNARDA. He went on a journey.

MARTIRIO (*looking at* ADELA). Oh, did he!

ADELA. See you tomorrow. (*Exits.*)

> MARTIRIO *has a drink of water and exits slowly, staring at the doorway to the yard. Enter* LA PONCIA.

LA PONCIA. Are you still up?

BERNARDA. Enjoying the peace and quiet. Strangely enough, I don't see any trace of this 'very big thing' that you're so sure is going on.

LA PONCIA. Don't let's talk about it.

BERNARDA. Nothing happens here without my knowing all about it. Nothing at all. And that's because I keep watch.

LA PONCIA. You're right. Nothing is going on here. Looked at from outside. Your daughters are quiet and smile like porcelain dolls. And, oh yes, they live very quietly inside their glass cases. But neither you nor I nor anyone else can tell what's going on inside their minds.

BERNARDA. My daughters breathe easy.

LA PONCIA. All that is your business. You are their mother. I just look after the house. That's quite enough for me.

BERNARDA. You've changed your tune.

LA PONCIA. I know my place and I'm better off staying there.

BERNARDA. The truth is, you've nothing to say. There's no dirt for you to stir. If there was, you'd have stirred it up and invited all the neighbours in to watch.

LA PONCIA. I know more than you imagine.

BERNARDA. Does your son still see Pepe at four in the morning? Do the neighbours still go on and on repeating their silly little slanders against us?

LA PONCIA. No one says a word.

BERNARDA. Because there is nothing for them to say. There's no flesh for them to sink their teeth into. And all because I keep watch!

LA PONCIA. I won't tell you what I know because I'd be frightened of how you'd take it. But I'll tell you this: don't be so sure of yourself.

BERNARDA. I have every right to be sure!

LA PONCIA. A bolt of lightning could strike you dead! Your blood could clot and stop your heart beating!

BERNARDA. Nothing of the kind will happen here. Insinuate all you like; it won't make any difference. I'm on the alert. I'm on my guard.

LA PONCIA. So much the better for you.

BERNARDA. Naturally!

MAID (*entering*). I've done the washing up. Is there anything else, Bernarda?

BERNARDA (*standing up*). Nothing. I am going to my bed.

MAID. What time shall I wake you?

BERNARDA. Don't wake me at all. Tonight, I'm going to get a good night's sleep. (*Exits.*)

LA PONCIA. When you can't move a mountain, you're better off turning your back on it. Then at least you don't have to look.

MAID. She's so proud she just won't see. It's like she's tied a bandage round her own eyes.

LA PONCIA. There's nothing I can do. I wanted to head things off but now they frighten me. Hear that silence? It's the quiet before the storm. And it's brewing in each one of those rooms. When it breaks we'll all be swept away. But I've said all I could. What else can you do?

MAID. She's just so determined and she thinks everyone should be the same. She just won't understand the effect one man can have on a group of single women.

LA PONCIA. I don't blame Pepe. I don't think it's altogether his fault. It's true that he was after Adela a year or so ago and she was mad about him, but now she should have known her place and left him alone and not provoked him. He can't control himself. He's only a man.

MAID. Some people say he's spoken to Adela night after night.

LA PONCIA. They're right. (*Lowering her voice.*) And not just spoken to her either.

MAID. I dread to think what's going to happen.

LA PONCIA. This is a house at war. I'd like to sail across the sea and leave it right behind.

MAID. And all Bernarda does is hurry up the wedding and hope everything will be all right. I suppose she could be right.

LA PONCIA. No. Things have gone too far. Adela's got her mind set on something and the others watch and watch and never rest.

MAID. Even Martirio?

LA PONCIA. Especially Martirio. She's the worst of all. She's a poisoned well. She knows she'll never get Pepe herself and, rather than leave him to someone else, she'd rather kill the lot of them.

MAID. They're all as bad as each other.

LA PONCIA. They are women without men, that's all. And when it comes to sex, everything else gets swept away. Even ties of blood. Sssssshhhh. (*Listens.*)

MAID. What's going on?

LA PONCIA (*gets up*). The dogs are barking.

MAID. There must be someone in the yard.

Enter ADELA *in petticoat and bodice.*

LA PONCIA. Haven't you gone to bed?

ADELA. I want a drink of water. (*Drinks from a glass on the table.*)

LA PONCIA. I thought you were asleep.

ADELA. I was woken by thirst. Why aren't you in bed?

MAID. We're just going.

Exit ADELA.

LA PONCIA. Come on.

MAID. I'm worn out, Bernarda's kept me on my feet all day.

LA PONCIA. You take the light.

MAID. The dogs are going off their heads.

LA PONCIA. They won't let us get a wink of sleep.

They exit. The stage is almost dark. Enter MARÍA JOSEFA
with a lamb under her arm.

MARÍA JOSEFA. My baby is a little lamb,
    I'll take him to the shore,
    I'll give him my breast and bits of ham,
    A little ant will sit at our door.
    Bernarda has a leopard face,
    Magdalena's a hyena,
    Little baby, little lamb,
    Baa, baa.
    Let's go to the stable at Bethlehem.
    (*Laughs.*) The door will open all on its own,
    And we'll go and we'll sit by the sea,
    We'll build a little hut like an orange pip,
    And we'll live there for ever, you and me.
    Bernarda has a leopard face,
    Magdalena's a hyena,
    Little baby, little lamb,
    Baa, baa.
    Let's go to the stable at Bethlehem.

She goes off, singing. Enter ADELA. *She cautiously looks about her, one way, and then the other, and then goes out into the yard. Enter* MARTIRIO *through another door. She stays centre stage, anxiously watching. She also wears bodice and petticoat, and round her shoulders is a little black shawl. Enter* MARÍA JOSEFA *from in front of her.*

MARTIRIO. Grandmother, where are you going?

MARÍA JOSEFA. Why won't you open the door?

MARTIRIO. What are you doing here?

MARÍA JOSEFA. Escaping. Who are you?

MARTIRIO. Go back to bed.

MARÍA JOSEFA. I know you. You're Martirio. Martirio with a martyr's face. Why don't you have a baby? I've got one. Look.

MARTIRIO. It's a sheep.

MARÍA JOSEFA. I know perfectly well it's a sheep.

MARTIRIO. Where did you get it from?

MARÍA JOSEFA. Why can't a sheep be a baby? Better to have a sheep than to have nothing at all. Bernarda's got a leopard's face, Magdalena's a hyena.

MARTIRIO. Not so loud!

MARÍA JOSEFA. You're right. It's very dark. Just because I've got white hairs you think I can't have a baby. But you're wrong there. I'll have baby after baby after baby. One baby will have white hair and then it'll have another baby and another and another. We'll all have babies and snow-white hair and we'll be like the waves of the sea:

one after another after another after another. And then
we'll all sit down and we'll all have white hair and we'll be
like the foam of the sea. But not here. There's no foam
here. Why's it all so dark? It's all so dark here. Everyone
wears black. Everyone's always in mourning.

MARTIRIO. Be quiet!

MARÍA JOSEFA. When my neighbour had a baby, I
brought her chocolate. And then she brought me some
and I brought her some more and then she brought me
more and so it went on and on and on for ever and ever.
You'll have white hair but no one's ever going to bring
chocolate to you. I've got to go, but all the dogs keep
barking. I'm afraid of the dogs. They might bite me.
Will you help me? I want to leave the country. I hate
country. I want houses with windows and open doors.
All the women lie in big brass beds with their babies and
the men sit outside on wooden benches. Pepe el Romano
is a giant. You all want him. But he'll eat you up, eat you
up every one, because you're just ears of corn. No
you're not. You're not even ears of corn. You're frogs
without tongues!

MARTIRIO (*energetically*). Come on now, it's time for bed.
(*Pushes her.*)

MARÍA JOSEFA. All right, but will you let me out
afterwards?

MARTIRIO. Yes. I promise.

MARÍA JOSEFA (*crying*). My baby is a little lamb,
I'll take him to the shore,
I'll give him my breast and bits of ham,
A little ant will sit at the door.

Exit. MARTIRIO *shuts the door* MARÍA JOSEFA *has gone out through and moves to the door to the yard. She hesitates, and then moves two more steps forward.*

MARTIRIO (*in a low voice*). Adela.

Pause. She goes up to the door itself.

(*Loudly.*) Adela!

ADELA *appears. Her hair is loose.*

ADELA. What do you want from me?

MARTIRIO. Leave that man!

ADELA. Who are you to tell me that?

MARTIRIO. That is no place for a woman of honour.

ADELA. Perhaps not, but you'd love to be in it.

MARTIRIO. I can't keep silent any more. This has got to end!

ADELA. This has only just begun. I've had the strength to push forward. The energy and the guts that you don't possess. I've seen death. Here, in these rooms. And now I'm leaving them to take what's mine.

MARTIRIO. He's a man without soul. And you've stolen him. He didn't come for you.

ADELA. He just came for the money, but his eyes were always fixed on me.

MARTIRIO. I won't let you have him. He must marry Angustias.

ADELA. He doesn't love her. You know that as well as I do.

MARTIRIO. Yes.

ADELA. You know that because you have seen him with me. You know he loves me.

MARTIRIO (*desperately*). Yes!

ADELA (*approaching her*). He loves me. He loves me!

MARTIRIO. Stick a knife in me if you like. I don't care. Only don't tell me that again!

ADELA. That's why you don't want him to go with me. You don't mind him kissing a woman he doesn't love, and neither do I. As far as we're concerned, he could live with Angustias for a thousand years. But you can't bear to think of him making love to me because you love him too, don't you? You love him too!

MARTIRIO. Yes, yes. Yes! I want to say it. I want to get my head clear of all these lies. I want to say it though there's so much anger inside me I feel I could explode. I want to say it. I want to say it. I love him. I love him!

ADELA (*on a sudden impulse, embracing her*). I'm sorry, Martirio, I'm sorry. But I can't help it. Don't blame me.

MARTIRIO. Don't touch me! Don't try to soften me! We're not sisters any more. We might like to be, but we can't be. Now you're just a stranger.

ADELA. There's nothing to be done. Pepe's mine. Choke on it if you like. It can't be helped. We'll go off to the banks of the river and make love amongst the reeds.

MARTIRIO. You won't!

ADELA. There is so much horror in this house. I can't bear it any more. Not now when I've tasted his kisses. Now I'll be whatever he wants me to be. Even if all the village turn against me. Even if all the village point at me, point at me with their fingers of fire and try to burn me. Even if all the so-called respectable people in this so-called respectable village pursue me and hunt me down, I'll still stand by him. Openly and without shame. And I'll gladly wear my crown of thorns.

MARTIRIO. Don't say another word!

ADELA. If you like. I'll be quiet. We'll both be. We'll go and sleep. He can marry Angustias. I don't care any more. But I'll go off to a lonely little house and live there so he can see me whenever he wants to. Whenever he needs to.

MARTIRIO. No you won't. Not while I live. Not while I've got a single drop of blood in my body!

ADELA. You can't stop me. You're just a weakling. I'll step over you. I could bring a stallion to its knees, with all the power inside me. Inside my little finger.

MARTIRIO. Don't talk so loud. Your voice annoys me. I feel so much evil inside me that's so strong it could smother me. And I can't stop it.

ADELA. They teach us to love our sisters. But that counts for nothing now. God has left me. We are both in the dark and both strangers. I look at you as if for the very first time.

We hear a whistle, and ADELA *runs to the door, but* MARTIRIO *gets in her way.*

MARTIRIO. Where are you going?

ADELA. Get away from the door!

MARTIRIO. Get past if you can!

ADELA. Get out of the way

They struggle.

MARTIRIO (*shouts*). Mother, Mother!

ADELA. Let me go!

BERNARDA *appears, in her petticoat and wearing a black shawl.*

BERNARDA. Quiet. Quiet! Why can't I kill you with the anger in my eyes? How poor I am. How feeble and weak!

MARTIRIO (*pointing to* ADELA). She was with him! Look at her petticoat all covered in straw!

BERNARDA (*turns on* ADELA). Straw is a bed for whores!

ADELA (*standing up to her*). You've no right to condemn me any more! This is when your judgements end! (*Seizes her mother's stick and breaks it.*) So much for the oppressor's stick! Don't you dare come close to me. No one has any power over me now. No one but Pepe!

Enter MAGDALENA.

MAGDALENA. Adela!

Enter LA PONCIA *and* ANGUSTIUS.

ADELA. I'm his wife now. (*To* ANGUSTIUS.) Do you understand? Understand now and tell him you understand. Go out there and tell him. He will come in here and he will command. He's as strong as a lion. Listen to him breathe.

ANGUSTIAS. Oh God!

BERNARDA. Where's my gun? (*Exit, running.*)

AMELIA *appears at the back, and looks terrified. She just pokes her head round the door.* MARTIRIO *goes out to the yard.*

ADELA (*about to leave*). None of you will have power over me!

ANGUSTIAS (*preventing her leaving*). You won't leave here. I won't let your body win! Thief! Dragging us all into the dirt!

MAGDALENA. Let her go where she wants! We'll never see her again!

A shot is fired.

BERNARDA (*coming in*). No use looking for him now.

MARTIRIO (*coming in*). That's the end of Pepe el Romano.

ADELA. Pepe! My God! Pepe! (*Exit, running.*)

LA PONCIA. Did you kill him?

MARTIRIO. No. She missed. He galloped off on his mare.

BERNARDA. My fault. Trust a woman not to shoot straight.

MAGDALENA. Then why did you lie?

MARTIRIO. To spite her! I'd like to drown her in a river of blood!

LA PONCIA. You're wicked!

MAGDALENA. Possessed by the devil!

BERNARDA. Perhaps. But it's better this way.

We hear a thud.

Adela! Adela!

LA PONCIA (*at the door*). Open the door!

BERNARDA. Open. Don't think a door can hide you from your shame.

MAID (*entering*). All the neighbours have woken up!

BERNARDA (*in a low voice, but still like a roar*). Open up, before I break down the door!

Pause. Everyone remains in total silence.

Adela!

She steps back from the door.

Break down the door!

LA PONCIA *gives the door a shove and goes in. On entering, she lets out a scream, and comes back onstage.*

What is it?

LA PONCIA (*bringing her hands up to her neck*). God give us a better death!

The DAUGHTERS *recoil violently. The* MAID *crosses herself.* BERNARDA *lets out a cry and moves to the door.*

Don't go in!

BERNARDA. No. I can't! Pepe: you're riding home, galloping through the olive groves, knowing that no one will harm you. But another day will come, and that day you will fall. Cut her down! My daughter died a virgin! Lie her on her bed and dress her in white. As a virgin! She dies a virgin! Tell the sexton to ring the funeral bell at dawn.

MARTIRIO. I envy her. She had him!

BERNARDA. No tears. Death has to be looked straight in the eye. Silence! (*To another* DAUGHTER.) I said silence! (*To another* DAUGHTER.) Save your tears for when you're alone. We'll all drown in a sea of mourning! She was the youngest daughter of Bernarda Alba and she died a virgin. Do you hear me? Silence, silence, I said! Silence!

Curtain.

The End.

19th June 1936

Translator's Note

Lorca was shot by the fascist authorities of Granada two months later. He was thirty-eight years old.